普及版

アメリカ人が語る アメリカが隠しておきたい日本の歴史

マックス・フォン・シュラー　著

ハート出版

Introduction
はじめに

When you read about Japan and the Pacific War in English, you will find much deep-rooted criticism of Japan. You will find statements like "mainline historians agree that Japan coerced 200,000 Korean women to be sex slaves".

日本や大東亜戦争について書かれた洋書を読むと、日本に対する根強い批判ばかりが目につきます。よくこんな文章を見かけます。「主な歴史学者は、日本が 20 万人もの朝鮮人女性を強制的に性奴隷にしたと考えている」

But I am different. Why? Nearly all of these English-language historians are Americans. They use present-day America as the standard for the world, and they really mean that America is the most perfect society in the world.

しかし、私はそう思いません。なぜなら、そういう英語圏の歴史学者は、ほとんどがアメリカ人だからです。彼らは現代のアメリカを世界基準だと思っており、アメリカが世界で最も完璧な世界だと実際信じています。

They think that if your country is different from America now, or was different from America before, it is wrong, and must be corrected. That is why so many Western historians, mostly American, criticize Japan about the "Comfort Women" system.

もしも、あなたの国が今アメリカと違っているなら、あるいはあなたの国が以前アメリカと違っていたなら、それはよくない、正さなければならない、と彼らは思っています。そういう理由で、多くの西洋人の歴史家、といってもそのほとんどはアメリカ人ですが、日本の慰安婦システムを批判します。

But the difference with me is that though I was born in America, I never thought, as they did, that it was the perfect society. Since childhood, I have always thought that Americans boast rather than work hard.

しかし、私はアメリカで生まれましたが、彼らと違って、アメリカが世界一優れた国だとは思っていません。私は子供の頃から、アメリカ人は一生懸命仕事するよりも、自慢することに熱心なように思っていました。

Americans expect to receive special treatment as a reward for simply being American by birth.

アメリカ人は自分がアメリカ人に生まれたというだけで、特別扱いされるのを当たり前だと考えています。

If you are a historian, teaching at a university in America, you dare not violate current social customs, such as Political Correctness (expression which means being politically fair and neutral and is also meant to prevent discrimination and prejudice).

今アメリカの大学で教えている歴史学者は、たとえばポリティカル・コレクトネス（政治的に公正・中立で、なおかつ差別・偏見を防ぐ目的の表現）をはじめとする現代のアメリカ社会の考え方に反する言動はできません。

Very unfortunately, political correctness has devolved into a form of oppression, it is now used to destroy the careers of people who Leftists disagree with.

非常に残念なことに、ポリティカル・コレクトネスは抑圧の一形態に堕落し、左翼が反対する人々のキャリアを破壊するために使われるようになったのです。

American Feminists have declared that the "Comfort Women" system was of sexual slavery, and that today's Japanese people must bear guilt for this. If an American historian wrote something different than this belief, he would be forced to lose his job in current America. Feminists would continue to apply pressure to his university until that historian quits.

アメリカのフェミニストたちは、慰安婦は性奴隷であり、今の日本人はそのことについて罪の意識を持つべきである、と断言しています。もしアメリカの歴史学者がこの考え方と違うことを書けば、現在のアメリカでは職を失います。フェミニストたちはその歴史学者が所属する大学に対して、彼が辞めるまで圧力をかけます。

I have spent a good part of my life outside of America. Since I am not employed by any educational institution, I write from a neutral standpoint. Many Americans would say that I have been brainwashed by Japan, since I have lived in Japan so long.

私は人生の大半をアメリカの外で送ってきました。私はどの学校にも雇われていないので、中立の立場で意見を述べることができます。多くのアメリカ人は、私が長く日本に住んでいるせいで、日本に洗脳されたのだろう、と揶揄します。

I fail to see how living in Japan for 49 years and learning the Japanese language well enough to write books in Japanese is brainwashing. I think that perhaps I have learned something.

私は 49 年間、日本に住み、日本語で本を書けるぐらい日本語を学びましたが、それが洗脳だとは思えません。私は、ことによると何か大事なことを学んだのではないかと考えています。

And while mainline historians accuse Japan of sexual slavery, American society was not so fantastic during the war. Just look at the situation of black people or the status of American women at the time.

主流派の歴史学者は、日本には性奴隷システムがあったと非難しますが、戦時中のアメリカの社会はそれほど素晴らしいものではありませんでした。当時の黒人の置かれていた状況や女性の地位を見れば分かります。

Japan is different, and took a different course. And in my opinion a superior course. The Japanese "Comfort Women" System was the best system ever in my opinion for solving the prostitution problem outside military bases.

日本は、アメリカとは違うしアメリカとは異なる道を歩んできました。私は日本の方が素晴らしい道を歩んできたと考えます。基地の周辺で行われている売春にまつわる問題を解決するには、日本の慰安婦システムは最善の方法だったと思います。

It seems that today's Americans like to pretend that their soldiers will not patronize prostitutes for moral reasons. This is not true, but scenes outside US bases around the world are often lawless and dangerous.

今のアメリカ人は、道徳的な理由で、自国の兵士は売春婦を買うようなことはしない、と思うふりをしたいようです。しかし、それは事実ではありません。世界中のアメリカ軍基地の周辺はしばしば、不法で危険な状態にあります。

I will also make some strong criticisms of Korea over the problems of the Japan-Korea relationship. This is not hate speech. It is my sincere hope that Koreans can solve their problems in their society without constantly blaming Japan.

この本では、日韓問題で韓国を強く批判していますが、これはヘイトスピーチではありません。私が心から願っているのは、韓国人が、自分たちの問題は自分たちの社会でいつでも日本を非難するといったことなく解決できるようになってほしい、ということです。

If one tells a truth, it is not hate speech.

真実を語ること、それはヘイトスピーチではありません。

マックス・フォン・シュラー

Contents
もくじ

Chapter 2 Were the Japanese Imperial Army and Navy really brutal?

日本陸海軍は本当に残虐だったのでしょうか？ ／*50*

Chapter 3 The Greater East Asia Co-Prosperity Sphere

大東亜共栄圏 ／*86*

Chapter 1
Was Japan an aggressor nation?
日本は侵略国だったのでしょうか？

What war means to Japanese people
日本人にとっての"戦争"の意義

Many international people assume Japan to have been a bad country during and before WWII, because Japan expanded into other nations. Well, it is not surprising that many people overseas feel this way, after all, since they fear Japan.

　外国人の多くは、日本は第二次世界大戦の戦中・戦前、他国にまで勢力を拡大したので、日本は悪い国だったと思い込んでいます。結局のところ、多くの海外の人は日本を恐れているから彼らがこのような考えを持つのは驚くべきことではありません。

But many Japanese also think like this, at least half, maybe more. Why? In America, I would guess the number of Americans who feel that America is bad for starting wars is less than 10%. And the other 90% of Americans look at them as crazy, naive idiots. Or as potential enemies.

　しかし、多くの日本人、少なくとも日本人の半分、いや事の依るとそれ以上の日本人までもが、そう思い込んでいます。何故でしょうか？ 一方アメリカでは、アメリカが戦争を起こして悪い国だと思っているアメリカ人は1割にも満たないと推測します。残りの9割のアメリカ人は、彼らのことをクレイジーで、子供じみたバカ、あるいは潜在的な敵とまで見做しています。

Why is this? Let us consider history. For many years, until the Meiji Restoration, Japanese people experienced next to no wars with another country. Now my foreign readers might be surprised at this. But the truth is that Japan did have many domestic wars, but they were basically fought by and within the warrior class.

これはどうしたわけなのか、歴史を見てみましょう。明治維新までの長い間、日本人は他国との戦争の経験がほとんどありませんでした。この本を読んでいる外国人読者は驚くかもしれません。しかし、実際に、日本では内戦は何度もありましたが、それは基本的に武士同士の戦いでした。

For the most part, the common people were not involved. Oh, to be sure, there were sometimes common people killed in the Japanese mediaeval wars, and were sometimes towns burned. These things happened when armies passed through provincial towns. But this was not the goal or intent of the warrior class.

基本的に、その戦いに一般の民が加わることはありません。もちろん、日本の戦国時代には、時には平民が殺されることも、町が焼かれることもありました。そのようなことは、軍が地方の町を通過する際に起こりましたが、武士が平民や町を襲うことを目的として行軍することはありませんでした。

They fought each other. And for the average citizens there was little effect irrespective of which party won and even when a ruler changed. Let us make a historical example. If Japanese had been like Europeans or Americans, and had thought like them, what would have been the result of the battle of Sekigahara?

武士は武士同士で戦います。一般の民にとっては、どちらが勝っても負けてもお城の統治者が変わるだけで、大した影響はありませんでした。具体的に考えてみましょう。もし、日本人がヨーロッパ人やアメリカ人と似ていて同じような戦い方をしていたら、関ヶ原の戦いはどうなっていたでしょうか？

Traditional Japanese postwar conduct
日本における伝統的戦後統治

The Ukita clan, which ruled the former Okayama domain or the present Okayama prefecture in Western Japan, sided with the Western Armies in that battle. The Western Armies lost to the Eastern Tokugawa forces. After the battle, the Ukita clan was sent into exile, and the Tokugawa clan appointed the Ikeda clan to rule the former Okayama domain.

西日本にある岡山藩、現在の岡山県を統治していた宇喜多家は、関ヶ原の戦いでは西軍に加わりました。西軍が東軍の徳川に負けてしまい、戦いの後、徳川が宇喜多家を岡山藩から追放し、最終的に岡山藩の統治に池田家を任命しました。

The citizens of the province did not resist the change, but accepted it. After all, it really did not affect them all that much. In case of a European war, the citizens were greatly affected. Most men of wealth and social standing were put in prison or killed. All property was confiscated. Many women were raped. If the former Okayama domain had been in Europe, people from the Ikeda lands would have held every position of wealth and power.

　統治者が代わっても、岡山藩の民は抵抗することもなく、そのまま受け入れました。結局、統治者が代わることは、民にとって大した影響はありませんでした。ヨーロッパの戦争の場合は、民に大きな影響がありました。富豪や社会的地位がある者は、牢獄に入れられるか、殺されました。財産は没収されました。多くの女性が凌辱されました。岡山藩の話に置き換えると、全ての富と権力に関わる地位が以前からの池田家領地の人たちに独占されたことでしょう。

Furthermore, people who had lived in the former Okayama or Ukita domain would have become second or third-class people. In that case resistance would have occurred. It would have been answered with massacres by the Ikeda clan. There would have remained deep-rooted hatred between the vassals and people of the former Ukita domain and the Ikeda clan.

　そして元岡山藩宇喜多家の領民は、以前より下位の二流三流の立場に置かれたことでしょう。すると当然抵抗が起きたことでしょう。その抵抗に対する池田家の対応は、虐殺です。そうなると、元宇喜多家の家臣や領民と池田家の間に根深い憎悪の感情が残り続けたことでしょう。

This did not happen in Japan at all. Japanese people simply did not develop such regional hatreds. And the truth is that after the battle of Sekigahara, Japan was ruled by the Tokugawa family with a military government, and that there followed a warless period of 263 years, which is quite rare in world history.

日本ではこのようなことは全く起こりませんでした。日本人は、そのような地域内での憎悪を生むようなことはしませんでした。そして実際に、関ヶ原の戦いの後、日本は徳川幕府が軍事政権を持って支配することで、263年もの間、世界でも稀な戦争のない時代を迎えるのです。

The truth of the Russo-Japanese War
日露戦争の真実

I think that many Japanese might feel that the Russian-Japanese War was a mistake, and that they should have let Russia take Korea at that time.

多くの日本人は日露戦争が間違いであったし、ロシアにそのまま当時の朝鮮を任せれば良かったのではないかと感じているかもしれないと、私は思います。

No. That would have been suicide for Japan. Why? Because the next target for Russia would have been unmistakably Japan itself. If Meiji-era Japan had not built a strong military in such a short period, Japan would have been taken by several foreign countries. England, America, and France would have quickly claimed Japanese areas if they had thought that it could be done.

それは違います。それは日本にとって自殺行為だったでしょう。そうすれば、ロシアが次に狙う国は、間違いなく日本だったからです。もし明治の日本が、あれだけ短期間に強い軍隊を作ることができなかったとしたら、日本はいくつかの国に支配されていたでしょう。英国、アメリカ、フランスは、それが可能と思えば、すぐに日本の領土を差し出せと要求したでしょう。

Why? This is the nature of foreign countries, especially Western white Christian nations. They thought that they must dominate and destroy other countries, and then use them for their own profit.

それは、外国、特に西洋の白人キリスト教国家の性質だからです。彼らは他国を支配し、破壊し、それから自分たちの利益のためにその国を利用しなければならない、と考えていました。

And with America, it is still the same today. In contrast, European countries have exhausted themselves after colonizing too much.

そして、アメリカは、今も変わりません。しかし、ヨーロッパの国々は植民地拡大をやり過ぎて、疲弊してしまいました。

But the fact of the matter is that in virtually all of Japan's long history, Japan did not invade other countries. There was only one exception to this, Toyotomi's invasions of Korea in 1592 and 1598.

しかし、ここで注目すべき事実は、日本は長い歴史の中で他国を侵略しなかったということです。ただ例外が一つだけあります。それは、1592 年と 1597 年の豊臣秀吉による朝鮮出兵です。

Many Japanese naively think that Japan was particularly bad, and should exist without a military. Without a Japanese military or Japan Self-Defense Forces, South Korea just might invade Tsushima like they did to Takeshima. Koreans are exasperating and annoying, but not yet evil. In English, there is a saying, “Power abhors a vacuum”. Maybe, “Power” can be changed to “National Power”. In America, it is understood in such a way. A weak nation or a weak man is swallowed by a strong nation or a strong man, and ruled by them.

多くの日本人が、日本は特に悪い国だから、軍隊を持たない方が良いという無邪気な考えを持っています。日本軍、いや自衛隊がなければ、韓国は竹島と同じように対馬を侵略す

A Russian cartoon. A country with the world's largest army and the 4th largest navy will stomp on upstart Japan.

ロシアの風刺画。世界一の陸軍国、世界第４位の海軍国であるロシアと、新興国日本には圧倒的な力の差があった。

るかもしれません。韓国は頭にくるうるさい国だが悪い国ではありません。英語で「力は真空を嫌う」という諺があります。「力」は「国力」と言っても良いかもしれません。アメリカでは、そういう意味です。弱い国、弱い者がいれば、強い国、強い者に飲み込まれ、支配されます。

Too many Japanese think that America can do no wrong
アメリカは悪いことができないと信じる多すぎる日本人

One statement that so many Japanese people make, when I describe the actions of Americans, is that Americans are so nice people that they would never do anything bad.

　私がアメリカ人の行為を評すると、多くの日本人が決まって言います、「アメリカ人は優しい人たちなので、絶対に悪いことをしない」。

There are several things to be clarified here. First of all, Americans, when first meeting someone, are kind and polite. It, however, is not true feeling, but just social graces. In general, Americans do not make deep friendships like Japanese people do.

　これにはいくつかの説明が必要です。まず、アメリカ人は初めての人に会った際には、優しく、礼儀正しいのです。しかし、それは真の感情ではなく単なる社交辞令です。一般に、アメリカ人は、日本人のような深い友好関係を築きません。

　And Americans can do very terrible things. Just look around

the world. But they think that they are doing good.

　そして、アメリカ人は非常に恐ろしいことを実行できます。世界中を見てください。でも、アメリカ人は自分たちが世界中で良い行いをしていると思っています。

Americans will always select and go for their own advantage. There is a Japanese cultural aspect of letting someone else profit at his or her own expense.

　アメリカ人は常に自分の利益になることを選択し、優先します。日本には、自分が損になっても、他者に利益を譲ると言った文化的側面があります。

For example, in a certain industry, there may be five companies. One company may willingly sacrifice its profit, so that all can flourish. In the future, the other four companies will compensate the one company in some way.

　たとえば、ある業界に５社あるとします。一つの会社が、それによって全社が豊かになるのであれば、自社の利益を進んで譲歩するかもしれません。そして将来的に、その他の４社が何とかその１社に対してお返しをするでしょう。

There are many Japanese people who think that Americans can be dealt with in this way, because they are kind. They think that Americans will someday reciprocate to Japan for Japanese kindness.

　アメリカ人は親切で優しいから、日本人と同じように取引相手にできると考えている日本人が多い。日本が親切にすればアメリカは将来的に日本にお返しをするとかかる日本人は信じています。

No, not at all. They may be mystified by the Japanese concession, or think that Japanese are stupid, but they will certainly take the advantage offered. And of course, they will never reciprocate. They will not see a need to do so or understand such thought.

　そんなことはあり得ません。アメリカ人は日本側の譲歩を不思議に思うか、日本人は愚かだと思うでしょうが、譲歩されたその利益はいただくでしょう。もちろん、将来お返しすることはありません。お返しする必要があるとは思いませんし、そんな考えを理解することもできません。

And I think that this is part of the reason that so many Japanese people seem ready to believe American propaganda about WWII. They seem to think that because Americans are kind, they will never tell a lie. It seems that they cannot comprehend that Americans might use distorted history to press their own advantage.

　これが、多くの日本人がアメリカが発する第二次世界大戦のプロパガンダを信じてしまう理由の一つだと思います。アメリカ人は親切で優しいから、嘘をつかないと信じているように見えます。こういう日本人は、アメリカ人が自分の優位を推し進めるために、歴史をねじ曲げて利用するという事実を理解できないようです。

The American way of propaganda
アメリカ流儀のプロパガンダ

Such is always the case with Americans. Japan is the only country to ever challenge the American world dominance. America, therefore, fears Japan. Its postwar propaganda about the Pacific War has two purposes.

アメリカ人はいつでもそうです。アメリカの世界支配に対して、戦いを挑んだ国は日本だけです。だから、アメリカは日本を恐れているのです。戦後のアメリカのプロパガンダには二つの目的があります。

One is to oppress Japan and keep Japan in a perpetual state of guilt. The second is to lie to themselves and conceal the atrocities that America itself committed on Japan.

一つの目的は、日本に圧力をかけ、永遠に罪の意識を持たせようとすることです。もう一つの目的は、アメリカの自国民に嘘を教え、アメリカが、日本に対して行った残虐行為を覆い隠すことです。

This concept of perpetual guilt is the way Americans deal with another people. You can see the same thing in how Americans conduct relations with each other. The problem is that too many Japanese take Japanese cultural nuances and apply them to international relations.

この永遠に罪の意識を持たせるという概念は、アメリカ人が他国民に対してよく使うやり方です。アメリカ人同士のやり取りでも同様のことが見られます。問題は、多すぎる日本人が、自分たちの文化的感覚がそのまま国際関係においても通用すると思っていることです。

In the heart of Japanese people there is an ingrain strain of giving way to others, and assuming that one's own group may be bad. Such is part of the profound Japanese culture. Japanese people will apologize quickly so as to continue amicable relations, even if they have done nothing bad.

日本人はお互いに譲り合い、自分に非があるのではないかと考えることができます。それが奥の深い日本の文化です。日本人は、たとえ自分に非がなくても、円満な関係を維持しようと謝罪をするでしょう。

In Japan, a country that is highly populated, this kind of culture helps preserve social harmony. But in international relations it is not good and, what is worse, may lead to a disaster.

日本は人口密度の高い国なので、このような文化によって社会の調和を維持し、守ります。しかし、外国に対しては、そんな文化は通用しないどころか、大火傷を負いかねません。

Americans, no matter how guilty they may be of wrongdoing, and even if they may clearly commit a crime, will always shift their responsibility or blame on someone or something else. That is why in American society they can have murderers who are obviously guilty, but say that they are not responsible for that murder and that there was something that caused them to do it, for example, their upbringing by their parents.

アメリカ人は、どんなに間違っていても、明らかに犯罪であっても、他人に責任を転嫁して非難します。ですからアメリカの社会では、殺人犯でさえ自分に責任はない、たとえば自分の両親の育て方が悪かったからだ、などと言います。

A recent case was the “Affluenza” affair. It means that a person grown up in an affluent environment, is spoiled and won’t be responsible for their actions. In 2013, in Texas, Ethan Couch, then a teenager, avoided prison with his defense. He was driving drunk, killed 4 people and injured 11 others. Instead of prison, he was ordered to rehabilitation. But he and his mother went to Mexico to escape rehabilitation, where he was arrested by Mexican police and remanded to the United States.

最近、アメリカで、「金持ち病」という言葉があります。裕福な環境で育った人は甘やかされていて、自分の犯した過ちに対して、責任をとろうとしない、という意味です。2013年に、テキサス州で当時十代のイーサン・カウチ少年が彼の弁護が奏功し刑務所入りを回避しました。彼は酔っ払い運転で、4人死亡、11人負傷の大事故を起こしましたが、裁判で、刑務所ではなくリハビリセンターへ行く判決を受けました。しかし、それを逃れるために、母親と共にメキシコへ逃亡したのです。その後メキシコの警察に逮捕され、アメリカへ送還されました。

Americans themselves recognize this, and there is a lot of arguing back and forth in murder trials.

アメリカ人自身このことを容認していて、殺人事件の裁判ではすったもんだの論争が盛大に行われます。

And this background is why keeping Japan in a perpetual state of guilt about the war is useful for America. It takes attention away from what America did.

こういった背景こそが、大東亜戦争で、日本に対して永遠に罪の意識を持たせることが、アメリカにとって有益である理由です。そうすることによって、アメリカが行なったことから注意が逸らされます。

American atrocities
アメリカによる残虐行為

The bombing of Japan by America in the war had no military purpose, and the US government understood it at the time. I think that it happened because of two reasons. One, the US Navy was really the most useful American military branch in fighting Japan. The Army was not really necessary at all once the Philippines, an American colony, were lost in this war.

アメリカによる戦争中の日本への空襲には、軍事的な目的などありませんでしたし、当時、アメリカ政権はそのことを理解していました。私は、空襲は二つの理由で行われたと考えています。一つの理由としては、日本と戦う場合、アメリカにとって実際のところアメリカ海軍が最も有効なアメリカの軍事部門であったからです。この戦争で植民地であるフィリピンを失ってからは、陸軍の必要性は実は全くありませんでした。

With just Marine Corps divisions, if America had increased the number of divisions from 6 to 10, the US Navy alone could have won the war against Japan. The proper strategy was the island-hopping strategy of going from island to island, and cutting Japan off from its resources in the south.

海兵隊の師団を、6個師団から10個師団に増やせば、米海軍だけでも日本との戦争に勝つことができました。正しい戦略としては、島から島へ移動し、南方資源から日本を切り離すことからなる飛び石戦略でした。

In America, the Army and the Navy fight over budget issues in Congress. Fist fights even occurred between Army and Navy personnel on remote island bases, over who could use the supplies when supply ships arrived to an island in the Pacific Ocean. The Army came up with its own strategy, which envisioned reconquering of the Philippines, and strategic bombing of Japan, to highlight the necessity of the Army in the Congress. But it was superfluous, and was not needed.

しかし、当時アメリカでは陸軍と海軍が主に連邦議会において、予算問題で争っていました。特に、太平洋の島で、輸送船が来ると、海軍兵・陸軍兵のどちらが補給物資を貰うかで殴り合いの喧嘩もあったほどです。そこで、陸軍が国会に自分が必要と見せる為に、フィリピンを奪還し、併せて日本を空襲する戦略を立てたのです。しかし、この戦略は余計なもので必要ありませんでした。

The second reason was that there were people in America that wanted to exterminate the Japanese people. There still are some today. America is a very racist and violent country.

日本本土を空襲した二番目の理由は、アメリカに日本人を絶滅させようと考える人たちがいたことです。現在でもいます。アメリカはとても民族差別の強い、暴力的な国です。

But virtually no Americans will admit this. So that if they can keep on forcing apologies from Japan, nobody will look hard at what America did.

しかし、この事実を認めるアメリカ人はほとんどいません。その結果、日本に謝罪を強要し続けていれば、アメリカの行った残虐な行為を誰も直視しようとはしません。

The city of Osaka was reduced to open fields by B-29 incendiary raids.

B-29による空襲で焼け野原となった大阪市。中央の通りが御堂筋、その右が西横堀川（現阪神高速）と四つ橋筋。

This may sound strange to many Japanese people, but defending your own country in conversations with foreigners is extremely important.

多くの日本人には不思議に聞こえるかもしれませんが、外国人との会話の中で、自分の国を擁護することはとても大切なことです。

Naive Japanese who do not defend their country
自国を擁護しない愚かな日本人

No one will respect you if you disparage Japan. They may agree with you, but in their hearts, they will think that you are mentally ill.

もしあなたが日本人でありながら日本を軽蔑する発言をしたならば、誰もあなたを尊敬しないでしょう。相手はあなたの意見に同意するかもしれませんが、心の中では、あなたのことを頭のおかしい人物であると見なします。

On August 15th a few years ago and after paying my respects to the souls at Yasukuni shrine, I went to a British friend's bar for some drinks. There were two people at the counter. One was a Japanese man in his 60's. The other was an American about 45 years old.

数年前の 8 月 15 日でした。靖国神社を参拝してから、英国人の友達がやっているバーへ行った時のことです。カウンター席に二人いました。一人は 60 代の日本人男性、もう一人は 45 歳くらいのアメリカ人男性でした。

The Japanese man kept saying “Oh Japan was so stupid to attack America!” Well, the American man, a friend of mine, said, “I don’t want to hear this!” and left.

　その日本人男性は「日本がアメリカに攻撃したのは本当に愚かなことでした」という発言を何度も繰り返していました。でまあ、そのアメリカ人は私の友達でしたが「そんな話は聞きたくない！」と言って帰りました。

You see, Americans will defend America no matter what. And even if Americans agreed with this Japanese man, they would think of him as feebleminded, and not ever respect him.

　アメリカ人は何が何でもアメリカを擁護します。しかしこの日本人の発言には同意しても、愚かな人物だと見なし、決して彼のことを尊敬しません。

Thus, no Japanese businessman or diplomat who makes bad remarks about Japan to Americans, and tells them that America is a better nation, is thought well of by them.

　そういう訳で、アメリカ人に対して日本のビジネスマンや外交官が、日本を軽蔑し、アメリカは日本より良い国だ、という発言したら、アメリカ人はその人のことを良くは思いません。

Oh, the Americans might use him, but they will easily throw him away.

　まあ、アメリカ人はその人を利用するかもしれませんが、利用価値がなくなれば簡単に捨てます。

The aggressive nature of white countries
白人国家の攻撃的な性質

Well, was Japan an aggressive nation? Not nearly as much as America and European colonial powers.

さて、本当に日本は攻撃的な国だったのでしょうか？ アメリカや植民地を持っていたヨーロッパ諸国と日本を比較すると、全然違います。

First of all, how did America force Japan to end its policy of seclusion? By military force and threat of war. Americans say that this was a good thing. Was it? I don't think so. Eventually, with the way events were in the world, Japan would have ended the seclusion policy in its own way.

まず、アメリカは、どのようにして日本に鎖国政策をやめさせ、開国させたのでしょうか？ それは軍事力を見せつけて恫喝するというものでした。アメリカ人は、それが良いやり方だったと言います。本当でしょうか？ 私はそう思いません。他国に開国を強要されなくても、当時の世界の状況を考えると、日本は鎖国を諦め、開国に向かったと思います。

But this is indicative of the aggressiveness of white nations, which is now only America. By their nature, they must conquer and dominate. They cannot let some nation live alone in peace.

しかし、これは白人国家の、現在はアメリカだけの、攻撃的な性質を示しています。他国を征服して、支配するのが彼らの本質です。他国に干渉せず、その国の平和な暮らしを放任するということができません。

Japan's expansion into Korea, Formosa, and Manchuria was of a defensive nature. When Perry's Naval squadron came to Japan, it was quickly apparent to Japanese leaders that if they did not develop a modern Army and Navy, Japan would be invaded and exposed to the risk of extinction.

　日本がその勢力圏を朝鮮、台湾、満洲に拡大したのは、日本を守るためでした。ペリー提督の艦隊が日本に現れると、当時の日本の指導者たちは、近代的な陸海軍を作らなければ、日本は侵略され、滅亡の危機にさらされることをすぐに理解

Commodore Perry's East India Fleet arrived in Uraga, Japan, and the next year the Japanese / American treaty ending seclusion was completed.

1853 年、ペリー提督率いる米海軍東インド艦隊が浦賀に来航、翌年日米和親条約が締結され、日本の鎖国体制は終焉した。

しました。

And to develop modern military forces, industry was necessary. To have industry, you needed raw materials. European powers were creating colonies across the world to ensure their access to raw materials.

近代的な軍を創るには産業は必要です。産業には資源が必要です。ヨーロッパ列強は資源を確保するために、世界中に植民地を作りました。

In such a situation, Japan needed to create its own colonies to maintain its existence as an independent nation.

そのような情勢で、日本は独立国としての存在を守るために、植民地を作る必要がありました。

The difference from the colonization by Western powers is that Japan annexed Korea and Formosa, and developed them into territories of the Empire of equal status with the home islands.

欧米列強の植民地との違いは、日本は当時台湾と朝鮮を併合し、日本列島と同様の地位をもつ領土に発展させたことです。

In Manchuria, they created an allied state. Here is where Japan was different from white colonial powers. Those white countries, including America, basically simply exploited the resources of colonized countries. They built little infrastructure, and provided little for the populace.

満洲では、連合国家を作りました。これは、白人国家と全く違う新しいやり方でした。欧米列強は植民地の資源を利用しただけで、インフラを整えることもなく、植民地の住民のためになることはほとんどしませんでした。

Their goal was simply to extract profit. Japan was different. When I first came to Japan, Japanese society was very much more an equal society than America. The emphasis was that all citizens can live at a reasonable level.

白人国家の目的はただただ利益を絞り取ることでした。日本の目的は違います。私は初めて日本に来た時に、日本はアメリカよりも、はるかに平等な社会でした。ほとんどの国民が、そこそこ満足できる水準の生活を送ることができました。

Americans take another approach. In America, the winner takes everything, and the loser does not survive. This is another reason white countries fear and hate Japan.

アメリカ人はそれとは違う社会を作ります。アメリカでは、勝者が全ての財産を所有し、敗者は生き残れません。これが、白人の国々が日本を憎み、恐れているもう一つの理由です。

The true meaning of colonialism
植民地主義の本当の意味

I have heard that some Japanese people believe America to be a benign nation, and that in Japanese schools, Perry’s visit is taught as a polite “door knock”. Not at all. It was an explicit military threat.

日本人の中にはアメリカは優しい国であると信じる向きがあり、日本の学校では、ペリー提督は礼儀正しく訪問したと教えられているということを聞きました。全然違います。軍事力による明確な恫喝でした。

America, like its ancestral European nations, was an aggressive expansionist nation. America would not let the American Indians exist, and they were nearly wiped out. Today, only remnants survive. America offered “help” to free the Philippines from Spain. Yet after the short Spanish American war, the Philippine people discovered to their dismay that the meaning of that help was American colonization.

アメリカは、その先祖のヨーロッパ諸国と同様、攻撃的で拡張主義的な国でした。アメリカの白人たちはアメリカインディアンの存在を許さず、絶滅寸前まで追い込みました。現在、アメリカインディアンは少数しか残っていません。フィリピンに対しては、スペインから独立するための「援助」を提供しました。しかし、米西戦争が短期間で終わると、フィリピン人は、アメリカの言うヘルプは、アメリカの植民地になるという意味だと分かり驚倒しました。

America certainly intended to dominate Japan for their own profit. It is what Americans do, and it is their nature.

アメリカは自国の利益のために日本を支配することを考えていました。今も同じ考えであり、それが彼らの本心です。

Many people in Japan today still do not understand the true meaning of colonization. What it means is that all the resources of the colonized country are taken from that nation into the country of the colonizer.

現在、多くの日本人は植民地化の本当の意味を理解していません。植民地になるということは、植民地にされた国の資源が、宗主国に全て巻き上げられる、ということです。

In Japan's case, I think that we can say that the greatest resource of Japan is the hard working and innovative population. If America had colonized Japan, Japanese people would have worked like slaves for American companies.

American Indians massacred at Wounded Knee. They were killed by the US 7th Cavalry Regiment. Seventeen men from the 7th Cavalry Regiment were decorated the Medal of Honor for this action.

ウンデット・ニーで起きたインディアン虐殺。虐殺を実行した第７騎兵隊の 17 名が名誉勲章を授与された。

日本の場合、一番大切な資源は、一生懸命働く日本国民であると、我々は言ってよいと私は考えます。もしアメリカが日本を植民地にしていたら、日本人は奴隷のようにアメリカ企業のために働いていたことでしょう。

That means a miserable life with no pleasures and no freedoms of any kind.

それは、いかなる楽しみもいかなる種類の自由もない惨めな人生です。

Americans always talk about spreading freedom, but this is not true. If you really want to understand the truth of this, just look at American society today. The truth is that the American way of life has become one of the most miserable among the First World nations.

アメリカ人はいつも自由を拡げていく話をしますが、それは真実ではありません。もし実情を理解したいのならば、現在のアメリカ社会を見てください。第一世界諸国の中で、アメリカがその生活が最も惨めな国々の一国になったというのが現実なのです。

European countries, if they had colonized Japan, would have been just as cruel as America. It was the nature of the times.

もしヨーロッパのどこかの国が日本を植民地にしたならば、アメリカと変わらない残酷な行為に及んだでしょう。残念ながらそれがその時代の空気でした。

Today, most Europeans have a decent life. In particular, European governments generally adopt something like the Japanese National Health Insurance Program.

現在のヨーロッパ人のほとんどはかなり良い生活をしています。特に、ヨーロッパでは日本の国民健康保険のようなものを採用しています。

My ancestral country, the ancient Kingdom of Prussia, had a system similar to the Japanese National Health Insurance. Prussia, being in the center of Europe, could not avoid being caught up in wars that broke out across the continent. Thus, Prussia needed a strong army to survive. If the population was not healthy, the army could not be strong. That is why a state health care system was created.

私の先祖の国、プロイセン王国では日本の国民健康保険のようなシステムがありました。プロイセン王国はヨーロッパの中心部にあり、戦争が欧州大陸のあちこちで起こると必ず巻き込まれ、避けることができませんでした。そのため、生き残るためには強い陸軍が必要でした。国民が健康でなければ、強い陸軍は作れません。それで、国による健康管理システムが作られたのでした。

America has a different approach. It is more important in America that a few people become extremely wealthy. Accordingly, their health care system is designed to transfer wealth from the populace to a few individuals. The American people have until recently put up with this system. The reason is because Americans used to believe that every person had the chance to become rich and powerful.

アメリカのやり方は、これとは異なります。数人が大金持ちになることがより重要で、健康保険システムは国民の財産を、その数人に吸い取らせるために作られました。最近まで、アメリカ国民はこのシステムを我慢していました。一般のアメリカ人は、だれでもが大金持ちや権力者になる可能性があると信じていたからです。

Now they realize that that is not possible, and this is the reason for the chaos of the 2016 presidential election. And the truth is that American citizens in general are not provided with adequate social security by their own country.

現在、アメリカ国民はその可能性がないことを理解しました。それが、2016年の大統領選の混乱の原因です。そして実際に、アメリカの一般的な国民は、国からまともな社会保障を受けていないのです。

Since such is the case with Americans in America, it is certain that if America had colonized Japan, Japanese people would have been treated horribly.

アメリカは、アメリカ人に対してそうなのですから、もしアメリカが日本を植民地にしていたら、日本人にひどい扱いをしたのは間違いありません。

The concept that Japan was somehow bad for expanding into other countries is simply American propaganda. And the fact is that Japan did not simply exploit other nations, but Japan developed them into a status that equaled its own level.

日本が他国にまで領土を拡張した悪い国であるという考えは、アメリカのプロパガンダに過ぎません。日本は他国をただ開発したのではなく、日本本国と同じレベルに発展させた、というのが真実なのです。

This was unique among countries that colonized other countries, and the uniqueness caused great fear in America. For this reason, Americans have had a need to continue to demonize Japan forever.

これは植民地を有する国々の中では特異なことで、アメリカ人はその日本の特異性をとても恐れました。それで、アメリカ人は永遠に日本を悪者扱いにし続ける必要があったのです。

The truth of the Japan-Germany-Italy alliance
日独伊三国同盟の真実

There is another serious reason that Americans regard Japan as an aggressive nation. That is the Tripartite Pact between Japan, Nazi Germany, and Italy.

アメリカ人が日本は攻撃的な国であると考える、もう一つの大きな理由があります。それは、日独伊三国同盟です。

Americans say that Japan allied with Nazi Germany. When Americans say alliance, they think of the WWII alliance between Great Britain and America. There are many photos of Prime Minster Churchill and President Roosevelt in conference, and even joking together.

アメリカ人は、日本はナチスドイツの同盟国だったと言います。アメリカ人が同盟と言う場合、第二次世界大戦の英米同盟を考えます。英国のチャーチル首相とアメリカのルーズベルト大統領が協議中で、冗談を言いあっている写真がたくさんあります。

Japanese Prime Minister Tojo Hideki never met Hitler or Mussolini. Military cooperation between the countries was minimal. If Japan and Germany were truly allies like America and Great Britain, then Japan would have invaded the Soviet Union in Siberia to help Germany in 1941.

Roosevelt and Churchill in the Atlantic Conference. It was held on the British battleship Prince of Wales four months before America entered the war. American military aid to Britain and the postwar world order were discussed.

ルーズベルト大統領とチャーチル首相による大西洋会談。米国が参戦する４ヵ月前に英戦艦プリンス・オブ・ウェールズ艦上で行われたこの会談で、米国の英国に対する軍事支援や戦後の世界構想について話し合われた。

日本の東條英機首相はヒットラーやムッソリーニと会ったことがありません。軍事的な協力はほとんどありませんでした。もし日独が米英のような本当の軍事同盟だったとしたら、日本はドイツを支援するために、1941年にシベリアに侵攻したでしょう。

It was not in Japan's interest, so Japan did not. When Tojo Hideki was the chief of staff of the Kwantung Army or Japanese Imperial Army in Manchuria, he refused Hitler's demand to return Jewish refugees to Europe, and let them settle in Chinese areas under Japanese control. About 20,000 Jewish people survived in this way.

ソ連への侵攻は日本の国益にはならなかったから、日本は攻撃をしませんでした。東條英機は満洲で関東軍の参謀長だった時に、ヒットラーのユダヤ人難民返還の要求を拒否しました。東條英機のおかげで、そのユダヤ人難民は中国の日本支配地域で生活できたのです。それによって、約２万人のユダヤ人の命が救われました。

But the Jewish holocaust is the reason for much Japan bashing today. People assume that since Japan and Germany were allies, Japan was as evil as Nazi Germany.

しかし、ユダヤ人の大量虐殺は現在のジャパンバッシングの大きな理由になっています。日本とドイツは同盟国でしたから、世界の人々は当然日本もナチスドイツと同じような邪悪な国だったと考えます。

The Nazi German holocaust of killing Jews was an awful thing, perhaps one of the most awful horrors of human history. Even today, it haunts people, and they cannot make sense of it.

ナチスドイツのユダヤ人の大量虐殺は恐ろしいことでした。もしかしたら人類の歴史の中で最もひどい戦慄的なことであったかもしれません。現在でさえ、そのことが人々を絶えず悩まし、何が何だか分からないでいます。

But Japan's conduct in the war was in no way to be compared with Nazi Germany. In fact, the Imperial Japanese military had more discipline and better conduct towards civilians than most American troops.

しかし、大東亜戦争での日本軍の行動は、ナチスドイツと比較すべきものではありません。実際に、大日本帝国の軍隊は、大多数のアメリカ兵より統制が取れていて、一般人に対して、より品行方正でした。

There is one important aspect that Nazi Germany and Japan did cooperate on though. When Japan attacked the American fleet at Pearl Harbor, an Indian revolutionary, Chandra Bose, was in exile in Germany.

それでも、ナチスドイツと日本の協力で、一つ重要なことがあります。日本が真珠湾のアメリカ艦隊を攻撃した時、インド人革命家、チャンドラ・ボースはドイツに亡命中でした。

He took a German submarine to the Indian Ocean, where he transferred to a Japanese submarine. He helped form the Indian

National Army from captured Indian troops of the British army in Singapore. They fought together with Japan as allies.

彼はドイツの潜水艦でインド洋にやってきて、日本の潜水艦に移乗しました。そして彼はシンガポールで捕虜となっていた英国軍のインド兵たちを集めてインド国民軍を創り、日本の同盟軍として戦いました。

This was an act that was most instrumental in achieving Indian independence after the war.

Chandra Bose on the conning tower of the submarine I-29, which is docked at Penang. In the center is the commander of the 14th submarine flotilla, captain Teraoka Masao.

ペナンに入港した伊号第 29 潜水艦の艦橋に立つチャンドラ・ボース。
中央は第 14 潜水隊司令寺岡正雄大佐。

これは戦後にインド独立を勝ち取るのに非常に重要なことでした。

The only other way in which Japan and Nazi Germany cooperated in the war was the "Monsun Gruppe" or Monsoon flotilla. A few German U-boats operated in the Indian Ocean based in Penang, Malaysia.

残るもう一つの日本とドイツの軍事協力には、モンスーン戦隊、ドイツ語で「Monsun Gruppe」がありました。数隻のドイツ潜水艦が、ペナンの基地を利用して、インド洋で行動しました。

Japan supplied them with fuel and food, but they could not use Japanese torpedoes. Thus torpedoes had to be brought from Germany. It was a long journey, and many submarines were sunk on route.

日本からは燃料と食料が供給されましたが、ドイツの潜水艦は日本の魚雷を利用できなかったので、魚雷はドイツから運んできました。長い航海で、途中で多くの潜水艦が撃沈されました。

This was the only joint military action between Germany and Japan in the war. You really cannot call that a military alliance in the traditional sense.

日独の軍事協力と呼べるのはこの程度でした。旧来の意味で軍事同盟と呼べるほどのものではありません。

Americans disregard good things for which General Tojo Hideki should be thought highly of, like saving Jews from Nazis.

　アメリカ人は、将軍東條英機を高く評価すべき事実、たとえば、ナチスからユダヤ人を救ったという事実を無視しています。

The true story of how the Japanese-American war started
日米開戦の真実

And the fact of the outbreak of war between Japan and America is that America deliberately prompted Japan to attack America. Any peace negotiation that Japan offered, America refused. Meanwhile, US Navy's intelligence department tracked the Japanese task force fleet as it approached Pearl Harbor. And they let it attack Hawaii.

　そして、日米開戦の真実は、アメリカが、日本がアメリカを攻撃せざるを得ないように仕向けた、ということです。交渉で、日本がどんなに平和的な提案を出しても、アメリカは拒否しました。一方で、日本海軍の機動部隊が真珠湾へ向かって進んでいることを、アメリカ海軍の情報部局は察知していました。そして、日本の機動部隊がハワイを攻撃するのを待っていました。

Even when Prime Minister Konoye Fumimaro offered to completely withdraw from China, America turned it down. President Roosevelt and Secretary of State Hull expressed some interest in this proposal, but Secretary of War Stimson said definitely that Japan could not be trusted.

近衛文麿首相が中国からの全面撤退を申し出ても、アメリカは拒否しました。ルーズベルト大統領とハル国務長官はその提案に関心を示しましたが、スティムソン陸軍長官が、日本は信頼できる相手ではないと断言しました。

Consequently, three and a half years of war and a devastated Japan, was it all better than negotiated peace? Most Americans today think so. They still think of Japanese people as untrustworthy and dangerous people who need American dominance to keep them from starting a war again.

その結果、戦争は３年半続き、日本は徹底的に破壊されました。それは、交渉で平和的に解決するより良いことだったでしょうか？　ほとんどのアメリカ人は良いことだったと思っています。ほとんどのアメリカ人の考えでは、日本人は信頼できない危険な国民であり、アメリカが支配していなければ、すぐ戦争を始めると考えています。

This was a very prejudiced view.

これはとても偏見を抱かせる考え方です。

In annexing Korea and Formosa, and in creating an allied state in Manchuria, Japan was doing what other European countries did.

当時の朝鮮と台湾の併合や満洲国建国で、日本はヨーロッパと同じことをしていました。

Many Americans still castigate Japan today. Why do they not criticize Great Britain or France for killing millions and world expansion? This is just simple prejudice.

現在でも多くのアメリカ人は日本を酷評しています。しかし、どうして英国やフランスが何百万人もの現地人を殺害して、領土拡張してきたことを非難しないのでしょうか？　これは差別に過ぎません。

Or even America itself for its past conduct. American history is blood-drenched. It seems that it is impossible for Americans to conduct foreign relations without starting a war.

それから、アメリカは自国の過去も批判しません。アメリカの歴史は血みどろの歴史です。アメリカは戦争を抜きにして、外交を進めることができないように思われます。

The problem is that Americans assume that Japanese people are aggressive like they are, thus they constantly assume that Japan will attack other countries.

問題は、アメリカ人は、日本人が自分たちと同じように攻撃的な国民だと思っているものだから、日本は他国を攻撃すると、彼らが常々思い込んでいることです。

Chapter 2

Were the Japanese Imperial Army and Navy really brutal?
日本陸海軍は本当に残虐だったのでしょうか？

Americans cannot comprehend Japanese people
日本人を理解できないアメリカ人

I am not an apologist for Japan. I am not brainwashed by Japanese people. This is what I hear when I speak with Americans about the Pacific War. They assume that all my years living in Japan has corrupted me. They assume that Japanese people have fed me with a constant stream of lies and untruths, and that my 49 years of living in Japan has caused me to forget American truths. They are quite sure of that.

　私は日本の擁護者ではありませんし、日本人に洗脳されているわけでもありません。私がアメリカ人と大東亜戦争の話をすると、こんなことをよく言われます。日本での生活が長すぎて、おかしくなったとか、日本人にいっぱい嘘を吹き込まれたとか、日本で49年も生活したせいで、アメリカの真理を忘れてしまったのだ、と。彼らはそう決めてかかってきます。

They assume that America is the center of all truth in the Universe, and nothing useful can be learned in any other country. Even if I were to try to convince Americans that there are many useful things in Japan by telling them that I am fluent in Japanese, that I write books in Japanese, and that I have many varied experiences living in Japan, they would dismiss all that as irrelevant.

アメリカ人は、大宇宙の全ての真理の中心はアメリカであると思っています。そしてよその国では有益なものは学べないと考えます。もしアメリカ人に対して、私が、日本語が達者で、日本語で本を書き、日本で生活していろんな経験を持ったと説明した上で、日本には有益なものがたくさんあることを納得させようとしたところで、アメリカ人はそんなことは関係ないと一蹴するでしょう。

And they would insist that what they say is truth; that Japan was a terribly brutal nation, and that a benevolent America modified Japan into a semicivilized nation today. But that Americans must constantly keep watch on Japan, otherwise Japan would quickly go on a rampage through Asia again.

更に、アメリカ人は、自分たちが言うことが真実であると主張するでしょう。曰く；以前日本はとんでもなく残虐な国だったが、優しいアメリカがその日本を半文明国に創りかえてあげた。しかし、アメリカが日本をよく見張っていないといけない、さもないと再びアジアでたちまち暴れ回るだろう。

Japan's rampage through Asia. This is a phrase I hear again and again from foreigners when I discuss the war in the Pacific with them.

「アジア諸国での日本の暴戻」。私は日本以外の国の人と大東亜戦争の話をすると、必ずこの言葉を聞きます。

Part of the problem is that Japanese forces fought to the death, and were extremely disciplined. This terrifies Americans. Well, the truth is that Americans are not really very good at devotion to a cause, especially today.

一つの問題は、日本軍の兵隊は死ぬまで戦い抜きとても統制がとれていたことです。アメリカ人にはそれに対する恐怖心があります。実際、アメリカ人、特に今のアメリカ人は、何かのために献身的になることが余りうまくできません。

I was a US Marine. We were trained to fight hard, and were trained to expect that many of us would die in combat. This was unusual for the American military. And many Americans fear the US Marine Corps, and try to destroy us by political attacks.

私は元米海兵隊員です。私たちは激戦に堪え、戦場で多くの海兵隊員が死ぬことを覚悟するように訓練を受けていました。アメリカ軍ではこういう訓練は異例でした。多くのアメリカ人が海兵隊を恐れ、政治攻勢でもって解隊しようとしています。

A Zero fighter plane equipped with a bomb swooping on the American carrier Bunker Hill on fire after a hit by another Kamikaze. Towards the end of the war, many young men volunteered for the Kamikaze Special Attack Corps, even though it meant certain death.

特攻機の攻撃ですでに炎上している空母バンカーヒルに突入中の爆装零戦。戦争末期、死が確実な神風特攻隊に、多くの若者が参加した。

Well, in most of American history, Americans have fought in foreign lands. They have had massive firepower, with which they could destroy any enemy.

アメリカの歴史では、ほとんどの場合アメリカ人は外国で戦っています。どんな敵も圧倒的な火力で粉砕してきました。

Am I saying that Americans lack courage? No. In the American Civil War, the armies of the South time and again beat the Northern armies in combat, though the Northerners were superior in the number of soldiers and the quality of arms. The difference was that the Southerners were defending their homes, while the Northerners were invading the South. The Southerners had much more motivation.

私は、アメリカ人に勇敢な心がないと言いたいのではありません。アメリカの南北戦争では、南軍より北軍の方が兵士の数、武器の質で優れていましたが、何度も南軍が勝ちました。その大きな理由は、南軍にとっては自分の郷土を守る戦いだったのに対し、北軍にとっては南部を侵略する戦いだったからでした。南軍の兵士の方が、はるかに強い危機感を持って戦っていたのです。

But Americans cannot understand the Japanese sense of devotion. Thus, they demonize Japanese. Americans take any incident, and exaggerate it. Whenever they speak of what Japan did, they always add adjectives like “brutal” and “uncivilized” to the conversation.

しかし、アメリカ人は日本人の献身的な感覚を理解できないので、日本人を悪魔化します。どんな出来事でもそれを誇張します。日本が行ったことを話す時は常に、「残酷な」とか「野蛮な」といった形容詞をつけます。

Americans are very good at propaganda and word games. They ignore whatever bad conducts their own forces did. A common phrase when referring to American atrocities is, “it was just a few bad apples”. It means that such atrocities were very few.

　アメリカ人はプロパガンダの使い方、言葉のゲームにとても長けています。そして彼らは、自分たちの軍隊が行った悪事は完全に無視します。アメリカ軍による残虐行為について、よく利用されるフレーズは、「痛んだリンゴもほんの少しはある」というものです。残虐行為はごく一部の例外、という意味です。

US propaganda about the Pearl Harbor attack, which exaggerates the despicableness of the attack and the brutality of Japanese.

真珠湾攻撃の卑劣さ、日本人の野蛮さを強調した米国のプロパガンダ・イラスト。

Well, the truth is that war is a horrible affair. In any war, terrible things are done by any countries' armies. Yet Americans will try to convince you that their soldiers were complete angels, while Japanese were awful devils.

　本当に、戦争は恐ろしいことです。戦争ではどの国の軍隊でも、大小の違いはあっても、ひどい行為が行われます。しかし、アメリカ人は、アメリカ兵は理想的な天使で、日本兵が悪魔であるということを信じこませようとします。

The opposite is basically true in reality. Japanese troops were highly disciplined. In general, Japanese troops behaved well toward civilians.

　真実は真逆です。日本軍は規律を守り統制がとれていました。全般に、日本軍は、一般人に対して規律ある態度で接しました。

Americans, on the other hand, were not at all disciplined. The Marines and a few elite Army units conducted themselves well with civilians. But the rest of the Army, and in particular support troops, behaved badly. Rape and theft were common.

　一方、アメリカ軍は規律を守らず統制がとれていませんでした。海兵隊や一部の陸軍精鋭部隊は一般人に対して規律ある態度で接しましたが、その他の陸軍、特に支援部隊にはひどい者が多く、レイプや強盗は当たり前でした。

Some of my Marine Corps experiences
海兵隊での私の体験

In my writings, I have written that I was an intelligence agent, and so I was never in a shooting battle. Well, actually one time, I was at the scene of an incident that was somewhat like a shooting battle.

以前の著作で、私は情報部局の人間なので、弾丸が飛び交う戦場には行ったことがない、と書いたことがありますが、一度だけ、銃撃戦の戦場に近い経験をしたことがあります。

I graduated from Marine Corps basic training in 1974. At that time, there was a Left-wing people's guerrilla group in California called the Symbionese Liberation Army, or the SLA. Their political goals were obscure, and they quickly degenerated into banditry. They were famous for kidnapping Patty Hearst, a newspaper heiress and the granddaughter of American newspaper magnate William Randolph Hearst.

1974年に海兵隊新兵の基礎訓練が終わりました。当時、カリフォルニア州にシンバイオニーズ解放軍（SLA）という左翼過激派がいました。政治目的がはっきりしないこの組織は、強盗を働くようになり、新聞王ウイリアム・ランドルフ・ハーストの孫娘、パトリシア・ハースト誘拐事件で有名になりました。

After graduation from basic training, I was assigned to school in Camp Pendleton California, halfway between San Diego and Los Angeles. When I arrived, the school had begun a few days before, so I was forced to wait for two weeks. The Marine Corps will always find a way to occupy your free time, so I was assigned to temporary guard duty in an area of Camp Pendleton.

海兵隊新兵の基礎訓練終了後、カリフォルニア州にある海兵隊の基地、キャンプ・ペンドルトンの学校へ行く命令が下されました。そこは、ロサンゼルスとサンディエゴの中間にあります。私が基地に到着した時は、学校が数日前に始まったところだったので、２週間待つ必要がありました。海兵隊では兵士に空き時間ができると、その時間を有効に使わせようとします。それで私は、キャンプ・ペンドルトンのある区域の臨時警備を命じられました。

It was an area right on the beach near the main gate. I was often assigned to guard the armory. Most guard stations in that area had only one guard at night, but in the case of the armory, we had two men. Well, that is because the armory is the building where weapons are stored.

そこはメインゲートの近くのビーチの上にありました。私はよく兵器庫の警備を命じられました。他の場所の場合はたいてい夜の警備兵は１人でしたが、兵器庫の場合は２人で警備を行いました。兵器が備蓄されている建物だからです。

There was at that time, and probably still is today, quite a backdoor trade going on in stolen weapons in America. Various criminal groups would steal them from the armory and sell them. Army and National Guard armories were very vulnerable, since they only had electronic protection. Meanwhile, everybody knew that the Marine armories were guarded at night by armed guards. However, we were only allowed to carry 5 rounds.

当時、おそらく今もそうだと思いますが、アメリカ国内で、軍から盗まれた武器が闇取引されていました。いろんな犯罪組織が兵器庫から武器を盗んで売りさばいていました。陸軍と州兵の兵器庫は電子警報システムを利用しているだけの脆弱な警備でしたが、海兵隊の兵器庫は夜も武装した警備兵が配置されており、そのことは誰でも知っていました。しかし、私が携帯を許されていたのは、実弾5発だけでした。

Well one night a message came over the radio that there was intelligence that the SLA was going to rob an armory in southern California that night. The guard force on the armory was doubled to 4 men. We were all just out of basic training, and scared and nervous.

ある夜、無線で、SLA がカリフォルニア州のどこかの兵器庫から武器を強奪しようとしているとの情報が入りました。私が警備している兵器庫に、2人の警備兵が増員され、全部で4人になりました。私たちは4人とも新兵訓練を終えたばかりだったので、恐怖で緊張していました。

On guard duty, there were 3 shifts. The two shifts at rest always slept in their uniforms so that they can be a reaction force in case of an attack. If we were in bed, and somebody screamed “Reactionary!”, in 60 seconds, we would be moving in a truck to the spot where we were attacked. As we ran to the truck, we were given an armored vest, a helmet, a rifle and ammunition.

警備任務は、三交代でした。休憩中の二組は、警備が攻撃された場合、応戦部隊となれるように軍服のままで寝てました。寝ている時に、上官が「応戦！」と叫んだら、60 秒以内にトラックに乗り、襲撃された地点に移動することになっていました。ベッドからトラックまで走りながら、防弾チョッキ、ヘルメット、銃、弾丸が支給されました。

We were often drilled in this maneuver. Well, that night with 4 men at the armory, we noticed the reaction force running outside the fence. Whether it was drill or a real attack, we did not know. Suddenly, we heard something moving among some wooden crates just outside the armory we were guarding.

私たちはこの一連の流れをよく訓練しました。ところで、ある夜、4 人が兵器庫を警備している時に、兵器庫の柵の外を応戦部隊が走っている姿を見ました。訓練なのか本当の攻撃があったのか分かりませんでした。そして突然、私たちが警備している兵器庫近くに積まれた木箱のあたりで、何かが動く音が聞こえました。

The rule was that we had to say “Halt” 2 times and then “Halt or I fire!”. Then if there was no response, we could shoot. And that meant shoot to kill.

銃の使用に際してはまず「止まれ！」と 2 回叫び、さらに「止まれ！さもなくば撃つぞ！」と叫びます。それでも止まらなければ、撃って良いことになっています。そしてそれは、射殺することを意味します。

Well, we were so scared that we all shouted it out really fast. There was no response, so we 4 Marines all loaded our weapons, and trained them on the crates.

皆は恐怖心でいっぱいで、すぐにその言葉を早口で叫びました。返事がなかったので、私たち4人の海兵隊員は銃に実弾を装填し、木箱に向けました。

It was a cat, so of course there was no verbal response. No, we did not shoot the cat, but it was close. I remember that I was very scared, and almost shot that cat. People who have never been in the military, or never been in a war, make many judgmental statements in a condescending manner about troop conducts. And of course, so do they about the Japanese Imperial armed forces.

それは猫でした。もちろん、猫は返事できません。まさか、その猫を撃つことはありませんでしたが、ギリギリのところでした。私が覚えているのは、非常に恐ろしかったことと、危うく猫を撃つところだったということです。軍隊経験のない、戦場へ行ったこともない人が、よく兵士の行動について上から目線で断定的なことを言います。もちろん、日本軍に対しても同様です。

But the fact is that in real war things are very confused, so you often end up shooting when you are not sure what is happening. But the truth also is that if you wait to be sure, you could be dead.

しかし、実際の戦場では、万事が混乱の極みです。このため、実際は、何かが起こっていて、それが何かはっきり確認できない場合でも、しばしば兵士は最後には撃ちます。しかし、戦場で、はっきり確認できるまで待っていたら、自分が死ぬことになるかもしれないのも現実です。

War is a tragic thing. No, I have not been in a shooting war. But that night, I experienced a little bit of the fear and uncertainty that goes with war.

戦争は悲劇的なことです。私は実戦経験がありません。しかし、あの夜、戦争に伴なう恐怖と不安を少しだけ経験しました。

Americans will never admit that their troops commit atrocities
米兵の残虐行為を決して認めないアメリカ人

One of the major reasons Americans today keep accusing Japan of brutality is to hide the truth of how badly US troops behaved in the war.

アメリカ人が、今も日本兵は残虐だったと非難し続ける一つの理由は、米兵が如何にひどい不品行を行ってきたかを隠すためです。

Americans will never, ever admit that their troops behaved badly.

アメリカ人は米軍兵士が行った不品行を絶対に認めません。

This is not something that most American people know. In fact, the average American thinks that the US military is the most wonderful military in the world.

ほとんどのアメリカ人はその事実を知りません。実際、一般的なアメリカ人は、米軍が世界で最も素晴らしい軍隊であると思っています。

But even today, you can read articles in magazines like “The Rolling Stone” as to how US troops in Iraq raped women and shot children for fun. They threw candies in the street. When the kids came to pick them up, they shot.

しかし、「The Rolling Stone」という雑誌の記事に掲載されましたが、現在でもイラクにいる米兵が女性をレイプし、ゲームのように子供を殺しています。キャンディを街の通りに投げて、子供がそれを取りにくると、その子供を撃つのです。

American troops pose for a souvenir picture with the skulls of dead Japanese troops.

日本兵の頭蓋骨を集めて記念撮影するアメリカ兵。

Well, the truth is that Americans cannot make very good soldiers. There is a certain aspect of the American character, where people think that it is good to always question people who are in authority. They think that this is a fantastic thing. They will say that they are not robots, like Japanese people, who act as instructed, but free-thinking wonderful people.

実際のところ、アメリカ人は良い兵士にはなれません。アメリカ人の特徴の一つに、常に権力者を疑うことが良いことだという考えがあります。アメリカ人はこの考えが素晴らしいことだと思っています。自分たちは、日本人のように、言われた通りに動くロボットみたいな人間ではなく、自分で意志決定できる素晴らしい人間である、と言います。

But the truth is that they are arrogant and obnoxious.

しかし実際は、彼らは傲慢で不快な人たちだ、ということです。

Arrogant self-centered Americans
傲慢で自己中心的なアメリカ人

I remember when I worked in a foreign talent office in Japan. They would supply foreign extras and people for Japanese films and TV productions in Japan.

以前、日本で、映画や日本のテレビ番組の制作のためにエキストラの外国人を派遣する、外国人タレント事務所で働いていた時のことを覚えています。

I was a location manager in that company. and found that most Americans were very difficult to work with. My basic job was to be a manager for the foreigners, and translate for them. Often with American people, they would start the day by telling me that they were not going to listen to any instructions from me. They would tell me that my job was to translate for them, and to give them what they wanted, like special food, or special rooms to stay in.

私はロケマネジャーを務めていましたが、アメリカ人は扱いにくい人物がほとんどでした。基本的に、私の仕事はその外国人たちを管理することと、通訳をすることでした。朝集合した時から、私の指示には従わないと言うアメリカ人がいました。その人物は私に、彼らのために通訳と、彼らが望む特別の食べ物や部屋等の用意だけをしていればいい、と言ってきました。

They were almost always very arrogant and egotistical. I would try to explain to the Japanese talent agency, but they would never understand. The problem is that Japanese people think that foreigners will work like Japanese. No.

ほとんどいつでもアメリカ人は傲慢で自己中心的でした。そのタレント事務所にそんなことがあったと説明しても、理解されることはありません。問題は、日本人は、外国人も日本人と同じように指示に従って働くと思っていることです。それは違うのです。

In America, people who behaved like that would be fired and sent home, and blacklisted. And that is how you need to deal with Americans, that is, by threats. The American workplace is a place of tension and conflict, so one never knows when he could be fired.

アメリカでは、そんな態度をとる人物は解雇されて、家に帰され、ブラックリストに載せられます。そのような威圧が、アメリカ人と取引、仕事をする際に必要です。アメリカの職場には緊張と対立があります。いつでもすぐ首になる可能性があるのです。

And that is why Americans in business and government are so arrogant and threatening to Japan.

そしてそれが、アメリカのビジネスマンや役人が日本に対して傲慢で脅迫的な理由です。

American-troops rape
米兵によるレイプ犯罪

But in a military situation, such an attitude makes troops behave like an undisciplined mob. In Okinawa during and after the battle, rapes of Okinawa women by US troops were very extensive.

しかし、戦時下において、兵士がそんな態度では、規律のない群衆になります。沖縄では、沖縄戦中も後も、アメリカ兵はたくさんの沖縄の女性をレイプしました。

During the occupation of Japan after its surrender, many rapes of Japanese women by US troops took place daily. While the Japanese government provided a prostitution service for US occupation troops, rapes were around 40 per day. But after the US government forced the closure of officially sponsored prostitution facilities, the number of rapes soared to 330 per day.

戦後の日本占拠期、日本人女性に対する米兵のレイプが、日常的に多数発生していました。日本政府がアメリカ兵向けの売春サービスを提供した期間も、米兵による日本人女性レイプ事件は、一日に約40件ありました。しかし、アメリカ政府が公的に後援されたその売春サービスを強制的に中止させると、一日約330件に急増したのです。

One incident that particularly upsets me is when three truckloads of US troops arrived at and rushed into the Omori, Tokyo, maternity hospital, and raped a large number of female patients and staff. One hospitalized woman's baby was trampled to death by the Americans. When some of the male staff tried to protect the women, they were killed.

私が特にむかつきを感じる事件があります。米兵が乗った3台のトラックが東京の大森にあった産科病院に到着し、米兵がその病院へ侵入し、大勢の女性患者と女性スタッフをレイプした事件です。この時、入院女性の赤ちゃんが踏み殺され、女性を守ろうとした男性スタッフも殺されました。

In Europe, American troops behaved the same way. The American Army in France and Germany simply raped and looted as they pleased. Many French people noticed that the German occupation troops in France were more disciplined than the Americans.

ヨーロッパでも、米兵は同様の行為を働きました。フランスやドイツで、アメリカ軍はやりたい放題レイプと略奪を繰り返しました。多くのフランス人が、フランス占拠期のドイツ軍の方が、アメリカ軍より規律正しかったと注目しています。

Yes, it is true that there was a guerrilla war in France during the German occupation. If, for example, the Maquis, the French guerrillas attacked a German military train, the German occupation troops would go into a nearby village, put all the people in the church, and set the church on fire, killing them.

ドイツ軍の占領下でゲリラ戦があったことは確かです。たとえば、マキというフランスのゲリラ組織がドイツ軍の列車を襲撃すれば、ドイツ占領軍がある近隣村へ入り、村人を全員教会に入れ、その教会に火をつけて皆殺しにしたものでした。

US troops line up outside the Yasuura house, a house of prostitution in Yokoska, Japan. To prevent Japanese women from being sexually assaulted by Americans, many such establishments for US troops were built.

横須賀の慰安所、安浦ハウスに群がる連合軍将兵。日本人女性に対する強姦を防ぐために、このような進駐軍向けの慰安所が各地に開設された。

But in basic daily life, the German Occupation Army did not bother the French civilians. And for the sexual needs of the troops, the German Army had their own prostitution system.

しかし、日常生活においては、ドイツ占領軍はフランスの一般人を構うことはしませんでした。ドイツ軍には自前の売春システムがあり、そこで兵士たちはセックスを処理していました。

Americans today continue to hide the truth of the war
アメリカが隠し続ける戦争の真実

Americans are very good at propaganda, very good at games of words. Even these days, too many Japanese people are still fooled by American propaganda.

アメリカ人はプロパガンダがとても巧みで、言葉遊びにも非常に長けています。今もアメリカのプロパガンダに騙されている日本人が多過ぎます。

Concerning the Pacific War, Americans say things like, “The Japanese people were deceived by a corrupt leadership”. Nowhere do Americans admit that they forced Japan into war.

たとえば大東亜戦争について、アメリカ人は「日本国民は腐敗した指導者たちに騙されていた」と言います。アメリカが日本を戦争に追い込んだ事実を、アメリカ人は絶対に認めません。

The atomic bombings of Hiroshima and Nagasaki are presented as being necessary to cause a crazy Japanese leadership to surrender. Nowhere do they write that the true cause of surrender was the Russian entry into the war. They do not write that the Japanese Imperial Army would have likely repelled an invasion of Kyushu scheduled for the fall of 1945, and Japan would have surrendered if then America had proposed peace terms acceptable to Japan.

アメリカでは、広島と長崎への原爆投下は、狂った日本の指導者たちを降伏に追い込むために必要なものだった、とされています。日本が降伏した本当の理由は、ソ連参戦だということに彼らは絶対に触れません。また、1945年秋に予定されていたアメリカの九州上陸作戦は、日本軍が米軍を撃退した可能性が高く、その時点で日本が納得する条件をアメリカが出せば、日本は降伏したでしょう。しかしそういうことも彼らは書きません。

Americans say that bombings of Japanese cities were necessary because there were many small factories located in Japanese neighborhoods. They do not say that the US Navy destroyed Japanese war industry by sinking 80% of Japanese merchant ships. With no raw materials to work with, the factories shut down.

アメリカ人は、日本の街には小さな工場がたくさんあったので、空襲する必要があったと言います。アメリカ海軍が日本の貨物船を約８割沈めて、日本の軍需産業を壊滅させていた事実には触れません。仕事をしようにも原材料がなく工場は閉鎖されていました。

The bombings of Japanese cities by America were nothing but genocide. And it was deliberately planned and prepared for. The American government built models of Japanese dwellings made of wood and paper in the Western American desert, dropped incendiary bombs on them and tested their effects.

アメリカが行った日本の都市への空襲は、日本人大虐殺に他なりません。それはアメリカ政府が、入念に計画、準備して行ったものでした。アメリカは西部の砂漠に、大部分が木と紙でできた日本家屋を再現したセットを造り、そこに焼夷弾を投下して、その効果を検証しました。

One of the bizarre bomb tests involved the bat bombs. Small incendiary devices were to be attached to live bats. The live bats would be then placed in a bomb canister, and dropped on a Japanese city. The bats would then fly and seek shelter in Japanese houses. When the timer went off at the set time, the bomb would explode, setting the house on fire. If a great number of this kind of bombs were dropped over a wide area, many fires would be started at the same time across a wide area, causing chaos and burning the city.

奇想天外な爆弾試験、コウモリ爆弾というものがありました。小さい焼夷弾を生きているコウモリに付け、それを爆弾の容器に入れて、日本の都市に投下するというものです。爆弾容器から外へ飛び出したコウモリは木造家屋の中に逃げ込みます。タイマーでセットされた時間に焼夷弾が爆発して、その家で火災が発生します。これを広範囲に渡って大量に投下すれば、都市のあちこちで火災が同時に発生し、都市は大混乱に陥り、焼失するという計画です。

But the bats burnt down the testing base in America, and this plan was abandoned by US forces. In any case, it was cruel to Japanese people, and very hard on the bats.

しかし、コウモリがアメリカの実験基地を燃やしてしまい、米軍はこの計画を断念しました。とにかく、日本人にもコウモリにも残酷な計画でした。

Americans approach war as a means to exterminate other people. Japan approaches war as a contest between warriors.

アメリカ人の戦争は敵国民を絶滅させるための行為であり、日本人の戦争は武士同士の戦いです。

Americans accuse others of doing what Americans themselves do. Last year, I visited a museum in Tokyo, concerning the Imperial Japanese military medical services. There was one exhibit, a model of a hospital ship. It was so clearly marked as a hospital ship that it could be identified as such day and night.

Skulls of many victims of Hiroshima some years later.

広島への原爆投下から数年後に発掘された多くの犠牲者の遺骨。

アメリカ人は自分たちがやっている悪行を他国がやっていると訴えます。昨年、都内にある日本軍の医療サービス関係の博物館を訪問しました。そこに、軍の病院船の模型が展示されてあり、昼でも夜でも病院船だとはっきりと分かるマークが付けられていました。

But despite this marking, which was according to international law, more than half of the Japanese hospital ships were sunk by America in the war.

しかし、戦争中、この国際法で定められたマークを付けていたにも拘らず、日本の病院船は、その半分以上がアメリカの攻撃で沈められました。

And America still does this kind of acts today. In the Middle East, there are many bombing attacks being conducted by America using drones. They will shoot a missile at some person, killing unconcerned people in the neighboring area. The drones will fly away, and circle back in about 30 minutes. They also shoot missiles at ambulances.

そして現在も、アメリカは同様の行為を繰り返しています。中東で、アメリカは多数の無人機を使って攻撃しているのです。ある人物を狙ってミサイルを発射し、その周りにいる関係のない人々も巻き込んで殺しています。無人機は現場から飛び去り、30分ほどで帰ってきます。さらに無人機は、救急車を狙ってミサイルを撃ち込みます。

Americans say that the ambulances are probably carrying weapons. When questioned by news reporters on why so many extra unconcerned people are being killed in drone attacks on suspected terrorist leaders, president Obama replied that anyone in the area near a terrorist leader is also a terrorist.

アメリカ人は、その救急車には武器が積まれている可能性があると言います。ある時、記者がオバマ大統領に、なぜこれほど多くの関係ない人々が、テロリストのリーダーと疑われた人物たちを狙った無人機による攻撃で殺されているのか、と質問したところ、オバマ大統領の回答は、テロリストのリーダーの近くにいる人物は誰でもテロリストである、というものでした。

The truth of the matter is that only 2% of the people killed in drone attacks have been actual guerrilla fighters. The rest are ordinary people. Americans invent new words to describe justly what their government does.

An MQ-9 Reaper drone carrying Hellfire air-to-ground missiles, which has been put into use in the Middle East.

中東に投入された無人航空機 MQ-9 リーパー。ヘルファイア空対地ミサイルを搭載している。

問題は、無人機の攻撃で殺害された人々のうち、実際にゲリラ兵だった者はわずか2%に過ぎなかった、ということです。その他の人たちは一般人です。アメリカ人は、このような政府の行為を正当化するために新しい言葉を創ります。

People who are killed in American attacks but are not targets are called "collateral damage". When waterboarding or other torture is used on suspects, it is called an "Enhanced Interrogation Technique". It seems that Americans feel that if they change the language, it will not make the actions so unacceptable.

攻撃目標ではないのに、アメリカの攻撃で殺害された人々のことを「副次的被害」と呼びます。容疑者に加える水責めその他の拷問は、「強化された尋問技術」と呼びます。アメリカ人は言葉を変えてしまえば、それらの行為がそれほどひどいものには感じないようです。

Yes, it does, because the actions do not alter their nature even if their naming is changed.

しかし、言い方を変えたところで、やっていることは変わりません。

The truth of the Nanking incident
南京事件の真相

When discussing Japan in the Pacific War, Americans always bring up Nanking and Manila as examples of Japanese atrocities. Well at Nanking, I am convinced that rape and killing did happen. But it was a battlefield situation, and this has always happened with all armies in history in some limited cases. There was, frankly, nothing unusual in this. War is so terrible an affair.

大東亜戦争中の日本について議論をすると、アメリカ人はいつも南京とマニラを、日本の残虐行為の例として持ち出してきます。まあ南京では、レイプや一般人の殺人が一部にはあったでしょう。しかし、これは戦場で起きたことで、歴史の中ではどこの軍でもこういうことが限定的事象としてありましたし、あからさまに言ってしまえば、異例なことではありません。戦争とはそれほど恐ろしいものです。

What is very unusual about Nanking is that the Japanese Imperial Army restored discipline after the battle. General Matsui Iwane increased the number of military policemen, and when Hankow was attacked, such an incident was not repeated.

しかし、南京の場合、極めて異例なのは、戦闘の後、日本陸軍は規律を回復したことです。松井石根将軍は憲兵隊の数を増やし、漢口を攻撃した時には、そのような問題は起こりませんでした。

And the Chinese KMT forces themselves, always killed and raped and robbed Chinese people. The commanders would not pay them, but keep the pay for themselves. When the troops became restless, the commanders would send them to nearby villages to rob and rape.

中国国民党の部隊は、いつも同胞であるはずの中国人に対して殺人、レイプ、強盗を働いていました。部隊長は兵士に俸給を与えずに、自分のポケットに入れていました。兵士の不満がたまってくると、強盗やレイプをさせるために兵士を近くの村に行かせました。

China is a very large country, and many KMT troops were fighting in areas far from their own districts. Thus, they would see nothing wrong with such behavior.

　中国はとても広い国ですから、ほとんどの国民党軍の兵士は自分の故郷から遠い所で戦っていたので、そのような行為に罪悪も感じなかったのでしょう。

This was America's great strategic mistake of the war. They felt that if they destroyed Japan, the grateful Chiang Kai-shek would become America's servant in Asia. Not at all, he barely controlled his own army, they were a collection of warlords with only nominal loyalty to him.

　ここで、アメリカは戦略的に大きな間違いを犯しました。日本を叩き潰せば、蒋介石は大いに感謝して、アジアにおけるアメリカの召使いとなると考えていたのです。しかしそんなことは起こり得ませんでした。蒋介石は自身の軍隊をほとんど統御していませんでした。彼らは蒋介石に対する名ばかりの忠誠心しかない、複数の軍閥の寄せ集めでした。

Chiang Kai-shek could not establish a stable China, or defeat the Communist Army. The Communists during the war treated the average Chinese peasant with respect. This great American mistake ensured that a Communist China would result. America should have cooperated with Japan to create a stable China.

蒋介石には安定した中国を作ることはできず、共産党軍に勝つこともできませんでした。戦争中の共産党軍は平均的な中国の農民を、敬意をもって遇しました。このアメリカの大きな間違いによって、共産中国の誕生が確実なものになりました。アメリカの正しい選択は、日本と協力をして、安定した中国を作ることでした。

It was after the war that the Communist party started the Cultural Revolution, and brought great tragedy upon China.

共産党が文化大革命を起こし中国に悲劇を齎したのは戦後のことでした。

But the Japanese military had a much better record than the US military. Americans cover up such bad incidents in almost all cases. There has always been much rape wherever US troops go. In fact, one third of female US troops themselves today are raped.

しかし、日本軍の実績はアメリカ軍よりもはるかに良いものでした。アメリカ軍がひどい事件を起こした時は、ほとんどの場合その事実を隠します。アメリカ兵が行く所、どこでもレイプ事件が発生します。実は、現在のアメリカ軍の中でも、女性兵士の約三分の一がレイプ被害にあっています。

How America evaded responsibility for the slaughter in the battle of Manila
マニラ事件はアメリカの責任転嫁

The battle of Manila is an instance of the case where the Americans blame Japan for what they themselves did. Americans have always said that Japanese troops went berserk in the city, raping and killing, and this is why so many civilians died in Manila.

マニラの戦いは、アメリカ人が，自分たちがやったことを日本のせいにした一例です。マニラ市内で多くの一般人が死んだのは、狂暴な日本兵があちこちでレイプや殺人を犯したからだと、アメリカ人は言い続けています。

No, such is not the case. The truth is that the American advance was very slow into the city. This was of course due to not only the fighting back by Japanese troops, but also American caution. Wherever American troops encountered a Japanese defensive position, they bombarded it with massive artillery and air strikes.

それは事実ではありません。アメリカ軍の市内への進入はとにかく遅いものでした。それは、勿論、日本軍の反撃に因るだけでなく、アメリカ軍の警戒心にも因りました。アメリカ軍は日本軍の防御陣地に遭遇するといつでも、そこを徹底的に砲爆撃しました。

This is what killed so many civilians, and while Japanese troops possibly did kill some people, they could not have killed 100,000 people.

それによって多くの一般人が死亡しました。その間、日本軍による殺人が何件かあったかもしれませんが、日本軍が10万人も殺害することは不可能です。

Only 1,010 Americans soldiers died in the battle. Clearly saving American lives rather than Filipino lives was a priority.

この戦いで、戦死したアメリカ兵は1,010人です。明らかにフィリピン人の命より、アメリカ兵の命を守ることの方が優先されていました。

In fact, the American conquest of the Philippines was very bloody. In the war from 1899 to 1913, somewhere around 1,000,000 Filipinos were killed. Waterboarding torture of Filipinos was common. Incidents such as the Balangiga massacre were common. This was a village where the American general was angered by Filipino resistance. When the American military first occupied the village, the villagers and US troops got along well. But after a time, the Americans began to take their food and sexually assault the women. The villagers made an attack killing

Manila ruined after being pounded by US artillery. 100,000 Filipinos were killed primarily by US air and artillery strikes in the battle. General Yamashita Tomoyuki of the Imperial Japanese Army was blamed for the deaths and executed in the International Military Tribunal at Manila.

米軍の砲撃で廃墟と化したマニラ市内。10万人もの市民が主に米空軍と米砲兵隊による戦闘中の攻撃の犠牲となった。マニラ軍事裁判では山下奉文大将が、このマニラ大虐殺等の責任を問われ、絞首刑となった。

many US soldiers. The US commander ordered that the village and surrounding area be destroyed. After the battle, he executed every male person in the village over the age of 10 as punishment.

実際に、アメリカのフィリピン征服は非常に残虐でした。1899年から1913年までの戦争で、およそ100万人のフィリピン人が殺害されました。米軍はフィリピン人をよく水責めの拷問にかけていましたし、バランギガ村虐殺のようなことはよく起きていました。そこは、フィリピン人の抵抗にアメリカの司令官が怒った村でした。アメリカ軍が最初にこの村に入った時は、村民とアメリカ兵の関係は良かったのですが、暫くしてアメリカ兵が村民の食料を盗んだり、村の女性に性的暴行を加えたりしたため、村民がアメリカ兵を何人も殺しました。アメリカの司令官は、その村とその周辺を徹底的に破壊するよう命令を出しました。さらに、戦闘の後、彼は罰として村の10歳超の男子を全員死刑にしたのです。

I was in Japan in the US Marines in 1974 to 1976. I remember that in 1975 we lost three Marines in Olongapo, Philippines, where there was a major US Naval base. A Major, a Sergeant and a Private were in a jeep driving around the base perimeter. In a remote area they were killed. The jeep and their bodies were left behind, but their heads were never found.

私は米国海兵隊員として1974年から1976年まで日本に派遣されていました。1975年に、巨大な米海軍基地があるフィリピンのオロンガポ市で3人の海兵隊員が殺される事件があったのを思い出します。少佐、軍曹、二等兵が基地の外辺部をジープで移動中に起きた事件で、基地から離れた場所で死体が発見されました。ジープと胴体が残されていましたが、頭部は見つかりませんでした。

Most Filipinos do like the US today, but not all. My command said that it was Communists. But is seems that some Filipinos are still angry.

　現在では、ほとんどのフィリピン人が、アメリカが好きですが、もちろん全員ではありません。私の上官は共産主義の人間がこの事件を起こしたと言いましたが、アメリカを恨んでいるフィリピン人がいるのは確かでしょう。

Do not be fooled by American propaganda
アメリカのプロパガンダに騙されるな

People in America sometimes wonder why Japan fought so hard in the Pacific War. They cannot understand why Japan did not surrender earlier in the war. To the American mind, Americans are a kind and gracious people, and so they cannot understand why Japanese people were afraid of Americans?

　アメリカ人は、大東亜戦争でなぜ日本があれほどまでに死に物狂いで戦ったのか、時々不思議に思っていますし、日本はなぜもっと早く降伏しなかったのか理解できません。アメリカ人が持っている自分のイメージは、アメリカ人は優しく、親切な国民、というものですので、日本人がアメリカ人を恐れていた理由が理解できません。

Americans, therefore, rationalize this by saying that Japan's leadership was evil forcing Japanese to fight. No. This is pure propaganda.

それでアメリカ人は、悪い日本の指導者が、日本人に戦うことを強制したと言って都合良い解釈をしています。それは事実ではありません。完全なプロパガンダです。

The American bloody conquest of the Philippines had only happened some 45 years before the Pacific War. Such incidents as the Balangiga incident happened many times. I am sure that Japanese leaders and people were aware of them. And the bombing of Japanese cities was genocide. These two incidents made it difficult for Japanese to trust Americans.

アメリカによるフィリピンの血まみれの征服劇が起きたのは大東亜戦争のほんの約45年前でした。その征服で、バランギガ村の事件のようなことは何度も起きていました。日本の指導者や国民はそんな事実を知っていたでしょう。そして、日本の大都市への空襲はまさに大虐殺でした。そういうこと

Filipino children being executed by American troops. This is from the New York Journal. The caption reads" Kill everyone over 10".

米国兵によるフィリピンの子供たちの銃殺。出典は『ニューヨーク・ジャーナル』。説明文に「10歳超の者は皆殺し」と書かれている。

があったので、日本人にとりアメリカ人を信用することが困難になりました。

After the war, Americans did not massacre Japanese people, while rape and crime by US troops have been a never-ending problem. Another major problem is that since the end of the war, America has been trying to remake Japanese society into one like America's.

　戦後、アメリカ人は日本国民を虐殺しませんでしたが、米兵によるレイプその他の犯罪はずっと続いています。もう一つの大きな問題は、戦後、アメリカ人は日本社会をアメリカ社会のように作り直そうとしてきたことです。

This is a grave mistake. American society simply does not suit Japan at all. Just look at the 2016 presidential election. At the moment American society is fracturing. It would be much better if Americans could be friends with Japan as it is, instead of trying to change and convert it.

　これは重大な間違いです。アメリカの社会は全然日本の社会には合いません。それに、2016年の大統領選を見てください、アメリカ社会は崩壊に向かっている最中です。アメリカ人が日本を変え、改宗させるのではなく、そのままの日本と真の友人となる方がずっと有益なことです。

Many Japanese do not respect their military
自国の軍隊を尊敬できない日本人

In America, to support the troops is natural like a religion. In spite of that, very few Americans actually do join the military themselves. But respect for one's own county's military is natural.

アメリカでは、軍隊を応援することは信仰のように自然なことです。とはいえ、実際に軍に入隊するアメリカ人は非常に少ないです。しかし、自分の国の軍隊を尊敬するのは当然のことです。

In Japan, we have an unnatural situation. It seems that many Japanese people have no respect for the present-day military, the Japan Self-Defense Forces, or for the Imperial Japanese Navy and Army.

日本は、不自然な状態にあります。多くの日本人には現代の日本軍とも言うべき自衛隊、それに帝国陸海軍に対して敬意があるように思えません。

This situation is not correct. It is because of the extreme efforts and sacrifice of the Japanese military that Japan has not become a colony of the United States.

こういう状態は正しくありません。日本がアメリカの植民地にならずにすんだのは、日本軍の血のにじむような努力と犠牲があったからです。

Yes, America does have strong influence and power in Japanese domestic affairs. But because of the resistance of the Imperial Japanese Army and Navy, they could not completely dominate Japan. This effort to dominate Japan was an ongoing effort since the arrival of Commodore Perry's squadron.

確かに、アメリカは日本に対して強い影響力があります。しかし帝国陸海軍の抵抗で、日本を完全に支配することができませんでした。アメリカの、日本を支配するという野望は、ペリー来航以来、ずっと続いていました。

And while President Obama's historic Presidential visit to Hiroshima shows that most Americans have deep hatred towards Japan, many in the US military have learned the value of military cooperation with Japan for the future.

オバマ大統領の歴史的な広島訪問で、多くのアメリカ人が今でも日本に対して嫌悪感を持っていることが明らかになりました。それと同時に、アメリカ軍人の多くが今後の日本との軍事協力の重要性を学びました。

I do not think that I can convince many Americans of the truth of Japanese military conduct in the Pacific War, but Japanese people should learn and understand that truth. And they also should convey the truth to for the people of the rest of the world outside America.

一般的なアメリカ人に大東亜戦争で日本軍が何を考えどう行動したのか、その事実を納得させることは私には不可能でしょう。しかし、日本人はその事実を学んで理解しなければなりません。そして、日本人はアメリカ以外の世界の人たちにもその事実を伝えるべきです。

Chapter 3
The Greater East Asia Co-Prosperity Sphere
大東亜共栄圏

Europe and America feared the Greater East Asia Co-Prosperity Sphere
欧米にとって脅威だった大東亜共栄圏

Americans in particular condemn the Greater East Asia Co-Prosperity Sphere. It scared them, because it was a political and economic organization newly designed to exclude the Western, White, Christian powers from economic and military domination of Asia.

アメリカ人は特に大東亜共栄圏を非難しています。彼らにとって、それは恐ろしい存在でした。欧米白人キリスト教国家によるアジアの経済的、軍事的支配を断ち切るよう新たに目論まれた政治的、経済的共同体だったからです。

These White Christian powers still do not properly understand what Japan did, so they demonize Japan. When describing Japan's efforts with the Co-Prosperity Sphere, they inevitably use adjectives like oppressive, brutal, or inhumane.

白人キリスト教国家は今も日本がしてきたことを理解しておらず、日本を悪魔化しています。彼らが日本の大東亜共栄圏での努力について述べる時は、いつも「圧政的」「残虐な」「非人道的」などの形容詞を使います。

Well, these things Western White Christian powers understand, because they did themselves in reality acts which can be explained as such. I will now describe how Japan behaved in a totally different way from the way adopted by the Western powers. One reason I can do this is by my own experiences in Japan, where I have dwelled for years. And another is because we have documented accounts of Japan's most stunning success, the annexation of Korea.

まあ、そういう形容を、欧米白人キリスト教国家はよく理解しています。彼ら自身が実際に、そのように形容される行為をしてきたのですから。これから日本の行動は欧米列強とは全然違ったという事実について説明します。どうしてそれをお話しできるかというと、私は日本に長く住んでおり、自分自身の経験があるからです。それから、実に見事な成功事例である、日本の朝鮮併合のことを記録した文書が我々にはあるからです。

Chandra Bose speaks before flags of participating nations at the Greater East Asia Conference in Tokyo in 1943, where leaders of Asian nations gathered.

1943年に東京で行われた大東亜会議。アジア各国の首脳が集まった。参加各国の国旗の前で、チャンドラ・ボースが演説している。

And the documented accounts are by Westerners themselves.

その文書は、西洋人自身が書いたものです。

First of all, what is a colony? It is basically a parasitic relationship between nations. The colonizing country sucks dry the resources of the colonized country. The only infrastructure that the colonizing country creates are the bare minimum needed to extract resources.

まず、植民地とは何でしょうか？　一般に、ある国が別の国に寄生するような国家間の関係のことです。植民地化した国が植民地化された国の資源を全て吸い尽くします。そして、その資源を吸い取るために必要な最低限のインフラしか植民する国は造りません。

Western-style colonialism. Aborigines restrained with collars.

欧米式の植民統治で、首輪をはめられた先住民たち。

Education, public health of the colonial populace is of little concern to the colonial power, as they cost too much. This is the capitalist system at its purest, drawing wealth from many to a very few privileged people.

その植民地の先住民に対する教育や公衆衛生にはコストがかかるので、宗主国は関心を持ちません。これは、最も純粋な資本主義システムです。数多くの人たちの財産がごくわずかな特権階級の人たちに吸い取られます。

Westerners created propaganda about colonialism, calling it "The White man's burden". They sincerely believed that they were doing good by going around the world, destroying the cultures and societies of people in various countries, and taking their resources and wealth.

欧米人は植民地での活動についてプロパガンダを作り、それを「白人の責務」と呼びました。世界中を駆け巡り、様々な国の人たちの文化と社会を破壊し、その国の資源と財産を収奪しましたが、白人は心から良いことをしていると信じていました。

From the Meiji Restoration, Japan sought to survive in such a harsh world. The first thing to do was to create a strong Army and Navy so that no Western power could take over and rule Japan.

明治維新以後、日本はそんな残酷な世界で生き残るための努力をしました。その第一は、欧米列強に日本が支配されないように、強い陸軍と海軍を作ることでした。

When expansion became necessary, they annexed Taiwan and Korea, and created a new state in Manchuria.

勢力圏の拡大が必要となると、台湾と朝鮮を併合して、満洲に新しい国家を創りました。

If America had not provoked Japan into all-out war with the West, and instead worked with Japan, and if Korea and Taiwan were still part of the Japanese Empire, and an independent Manchukuo still existed, I think it is safe to say that China would not be Communist today.

もしアメリカが、日本を欧米列強との戦争に追い込むようなことはせず、逆に日本と協力していたら、もし朝鮮と台湾が今も大日本帝国の一部で、満洲国がまだ存在していたら、現在の中国は共産主義国家ではなかっただろうと言っても問題ないと考えます。

The true nature of the Greater East Asia Co-Prosperity Sphere
大東亜共栄圏の真実

Having lived in Japan for 49 years, I know that Japan is an inclusive society. There is very little of the outright prejudice that exists in Western countries. People are expected to behave and act according to socially accepted rules. If you do this, you are accepted as a member of society.

日本に49年も住んでいると、日本は共生の社会であるということ分かります。欧米のように明白な偏見はほとんどありません。社会の常識に従って行動することを人々は期待されています。それができれば、社会の一員として受け入れられます。

Nearly every Westerner who comes to Japan does not understand this. They bring the baggage of "assumed Western superiority", which is really colonial thinking. They cannot compromise and do things the Japanese way, because of inbred ideas that they are naturally superior to Japanese or Asians.

日本にやってくるほとんどの欧米人は、これを理解できません。「西洋人優越が当然」という荷物を携えてやってきます。これは本当に植民地的な考え方です。彼らは、歩み寄って日本流に倣うことができませんが、それは彼らが生まれながらにして西洋人が日本人、アジア人より優れた存在であると思っているからです。

Thus, very few Westerners do well in Japan.

そんなわけで､日本で問題なくやれる西洋人は少ないです。

There was one thing which Western countries did, but which Japan did not do. That was to require military service of countries under Japanese influence. Some 11,000 Burmese troops who fought together with Japan, some 57,000 Indonesians, and Thais who allied with Japan, were not required to serve outside their home countries.

一つ、植民地において西洋国家が行い、日本が行わなかったことがあります。それは、自国の外での軍務を要求することです。日本と共闘した約11,000のビルマ兵、約57,000のインドネシア兵、および日本と同盟関係にあったタイ軍は、彼らの本国の外で戦うことは要求されませんでした。

Koreans were not required to serve in the military until nearly the end of the war.

朝鮮人には戦争末期まで軍務に就くことは要求されませんでした。

This contrasts with Great Britain and France, both of which made extensive use of colonial troops. Germany had allied countries such as Italy, Rumania, and Hungary send troops into Russia.

それとは対照的に、英国やフランスは、植民地で数多くの兵士を募りました。ドイツの場合、同盟国、たとえば、イタリアやルーマニア、ハンガリーに軍隊をロシアの前線へ送らせました。

Japan did not require the countries allied with Japan to fight outside their borders. The Indian National Army was used in an invasion of India.

日本は同盟国に対して、国境の外での戦闘を要求しませんでした。インド国民軍はインド攻略のために動員されたのでした。

But the Greater East Asia Co-Prosperity Sphere really did not exist long enough to prove that Japan did not exploit Asian nations, but tried to create an equal relationship with and among them. Instead, we can look for the proof of this in the relationship Imperial Japan had with Korea.

　しかし、日本がアジアの国々から搾取したのではなく、平等な関係を作ろうと努力したことを証明するには、大東亜共栄圏は短命すぎました。しかしその証拠は、日本と当時の朝鮮の関係を見れば分かります。

Let us examine this relationship.

　それではその関係を見ていきましょう。

The Imperial Japanese Army and the Indian National Army fight together.

共闘する日本軍とインド国民軍。

Chapter 4
Why can't the Japan-Korea problem be solved?
日韓関係はなぜ修復できないのでしょうか？

The cause of all the trouble is Korea
全てのトラブルの原因は韓国

I think that most people in the world today are aware of the deep acrimony between Japan and Korea. One thing I can say for sure is that it is all from the Korean side. Japanese people do not harbor such ill will as hatred towards Koreans, but are exasperated. It is the Koreans that express so much hate to Japanese. In the following chapters I will explain why this is so.

世界の多くの人々は、日本と韓国は根の深い、ギスギスした関係にあることを理解していると思います。一つ言えるのは、このトラブルは全部韓国側が起こしているということです。日本人は韓国人に対して憎悪というほどの悪い感情は持っていませんが、苛立っています。日本人に対して強い憎悪の念を表出しているのは韓国人です。この章では、そんな日韓関係についてお話しします。

First of all, it is not unusual for neighboring nations to have problems. When the Roman Imperial border stopped along the Rhine, it ensured centuries of rivalry between France and Germany. Both Hungary and Romania were German allies in WWII, and sent troops to fight alongside Germany in the war in Russia. Yet the German military command had to put Italian troops in between them, out of fear that they would fight each other.

まず、隣り合う国家間で問題があることは、世界の歴史をみても珍しいことではありません。ローマ帝国の境界線がライン川で留まったことで、ドイツとフランスは何百年間もライバルとして戦うことになりました。ハンガリーとルーマニアは第二次世界大戦では、両国共にドイツと同盟を結びました。両国は、ドイツと共にロシアで戦うために軍を派遣しました。しかし、ドイツの司令部は前線で両軍の間にイタリア軍を置きました。ハンガリー軍とルーマニア軍が隣同士だと、戦いが始まってしまう懸念があったからです。

Well, what about America? Ask any Canadian or Mexican what they think of America, you will get an idea how they dislike America. But there are some unique aspects of the Japanese-Korean relationship, and frankly this is because of the unusual nature of the Korean people.

さて、アメリカの評判はどうでしょうか？　カナダ人やメキシコ人に聞くと、彼らがアメリカを嫌っていることが分かります。しかし、日韓問題では、独特な様相が見られます。この原因は、率直に言うと、韓国人の異常とも言える国民性にあります。

First, I mention some basic history of both nations.

最初に、両国の基本的な歴史を説明します。

Korean history
韓国の歴史

The first known Korean state, Gojoseon, is said to have been founded in 2333 B.C. Various states thereafter existed on the Korean peninsula, until about the first century of the Christian era three kingdoms were formed. They were Goguryeo, which basically corresponded to modern-day North Korea, Silla, which was the eastern half of modern South Korea, and Baekje, which formed the western half of present South Korea.

朝鮮半島の最初の国、古朝鮮は、紀元前2333年に建国されたとされています。その後いろいろな国が興り、紀元一世紀頃に、三つの王国ができました。ほぼ今の北朝鮮に位置する高句麗、今の韓国東部に位置する新羅、西部に位置する百済、の三国です。

In 1392, the Joseon dynasty established itself over a unified country in the Korean peninsula, and it is from this period that we concern ourselves with present Japan-Korea issues.

1392年に李氏朝鮮が朝鮮半島に統一国家を打ち立てましたが、今の日韓問題については、ここからが重要です。

Japanese history
日本の歴史

The Imperial family of Japan goes back more than 2,600 years, and this was the first beginning of a Japanese state. But there is also strong opinion that the Jomon era could truly be considered the foundation of Japanese civilization. This era began about 14,000 B.C.

日本の皇室の歴史は、約 2,600 年前にさかのぼります。日本国の始まりです。しかし、実際に日本文明が始まったのは縄文時代からだとする有力な意見もあります。縄文時代が始まったのは紀元前 14,000 年からです。

Japanese culture and art gradually became more sophisticated through the Asuka, Nara, and Heian periods. After the Heian period, Minamoto No Yoritomo was a leading samurai, and a samurai government was born at Kamakura, and then a period of civil wars, called the period of warring states, lasted until the overwhelming victory of the Tokugawa clan.

飛鳥時代、奈良時代、平安時代と続き、日本の文化、芸術は次第に洗練されていきました。平安時代の後、源頼朝が武士の頂点に立ち、鎌倉に武家政権が誕生し、その後戦国時代と呼ばれる内戦の期間が、徳川家の大勝利で終わるまで続きました。

This was followed by the Edo era, a time renewed for the flowering of art and culture. The Arrival of Commodore Perry's flotilla in 1853 forced Japan under seclusion to open the country to the world.

その次の時代が江戸時代です。江戸時代になると、芸術や文化がさらに発展しました。そしてペリー提督が 1853 年に来航して、鎖国下にあった日本に開国を迫りました。

A political revolution formed the Meiji government, which then embarked upon an ambitious era of reform. A modern army and a navy were built, and Western efforts to dominate Japan were resisted.

政治的革命によって明治政府が誕生し、それから野心的な改革の時代が始まりました。近代的な陸海軍を創設し、欧米列強による日本支配に対抗しようとしました。

It was at this time that Japan annexed Korea after soundly defeating Russia in the war of 1904 to 1905. It is from here we will begin.

1904年～1905年の日露戦争で大勝利した後、日本が朝鮮を併合したのは、そんな時代のことでした。

The Yi dynasty class system
李氏朝鮮の身分制度

It was in the Joseon era that Korean antipathy towards Japan began. Let us see why.

コリアの人たちが日本を毛嫌いし始めたのは、李氏朝鮮の時代のことでした。その理由を説明しましょう。

Korea at that time was a very traditionalist Confucian state. It was divided into several social classes, and the top class was the Yangban or nobles. This rank was achieved by passing an examination in classical Chinese Confucianist literature. But since the exams were rigorous, and required extensive study, only those who could spend years in study could pass. In this way, the ruling class became basically hereditary.

その時代、李氏朝鮮は伝統的な儒教の国でした。人々はいくつかの階級に分かれていました。一番上はヤンバン（両班）、貴族の階級でした。この階級に上がるためには、科挙試験に合格する必要がありました。その試験はとても難しく広範囲な勉学が必要だったので、長い年月をかけて勉強できる人だけが合格しました。このようにして、この支配階級は基本的に世襲となりました。

Below this class was the Chungin, who became doctors, technicians and so forth.

その下は中人で、医者、技術者などでした。

Korean aristocrats play chess.

将棋を指す両班。

Then there were Sangmin, who were farmers, heavy laborers, fishermen, merchants and so forth.

次は常民で、基本的に農民、重労働者、漁民、商人、ほかでした。

And next was the Cheonmin, who were entertainers, butchers and shamans. Various historians may rank these classes differently, but this is a basic idea of their status.

その下は賎民で、芸能人、屠殺者、シャーマンでした。歴史家によって、この分類やランクは違うかも知れませんが、これは基本的な見方です。

Then there was a Baekjeong untouchable class, which included prostitutes, and below them were the Nobi, or slave class. Some 40% to 50% of the population of Yi dynasty Korea was this slave class. It was hereditary. Again, estimates of the percentage of slaves in Korean society differ among historians, but it was quite large.

次が、白丁といって不可触民で、売春等の人たち、一番下は、奴婢で、奴隷でした。李氏朝鮮の人口は、大略４割から５割が奴婢で、それはほぼ世襲でした。韓国社会でのこの割合も、歴史家によって違いますが、その人数はとても多いものでした。

Yes, there were slaves in Korea. In Japan, there was indentured labor, but never was a human being in Japan completely owned by another. And slavery still exists in Korea today. Recently, the British newspaper The Independent did an article about salt farms on remote islands off the southwestern Korean coast. They make salt from sea water, and it is backbreaking work. To get labor, they kidnap mentally disturbed or homeless people from Seoul and hold them as slaves.

　そうです。李氏朝鮮には奴隷がいました。日本では、年季奉公労働はありましたが、人間が別の人の所有物になることは決してありませんでした。韓国には現在も奴隷制度があります。最近の英国の新聞インデペンデントに、韓国南西沖の僻遠の島にある塩田についての記事がありました。そこでは海水から塩を作るのですが、厳しい労働環境です。その労働に従事させるために、ソウルから、知的障害者やホームレスを誘拐してきて、奴隷として働かせていました。

The local police are in on the deal, and so they won't make a move about it. If a slave escapes, the police catch and send him back to the owner. When Japan annexed Korea, slavery was abolished.

　その島の警察は事態に関与しているので、この問題について動きませんし、奴隷が脱走した場合、警察が捉えてその脱走者を所有者に返しました。かつて日本が朝鮮を併合した時、奴隷制は廃止されました。

Culture and literacy rate in Yi dynasty Korea
李氏朝鮮の文化と識字率

In Joseon Korea or Yi dynasty Korea, it was a state of extreme submission to the higher ranked people. Education for the common people basically did not exist, and so literacy rate among the general populace was extremely low. In 1910, at the time of annexation, it was estimated to be about 6% of the population. Even though King Sejong the Great published the Korean Hangul alphabet in 1446, its use was resisted by the Yangban nobility. They looked down upon it as low-class, preferring to use classical Chinese. Thus, literacy rate was low. The average life span in Yi Dynasty Korea was 24 years for men and 26 years for women. That is the same as uncivilized primitive man living in caves. We can compare this to Edo era Japan, where people could expect to live to be 50 years old.

李氏朝鮮は、自分より階級が上位の人には逆らうことができない、完全な階級社会でした。一般庶民の教育は基本的に存在しなかったので識字率はとても低く、1910年に日本が併合した時、約6%しかありませんでした。1446年に朝鮮王世宗がハングルを公布しましたが、両班階級からは反発されました。彼らは、ハングルは、低俗な文字だと考え漢文の使用を好みました。このため、識字率は低いままでした。李氏朝鮮における平均寿命は、男性が24年で、女性は26年でした。これは、洞穴に住んでいた原始人と同じです。我々はこれを江戸時代の日本と比較でき、当時の日本の平均寿命は50歳でした。

Except for the literacy rate and average life issues, in a broad sense, we can plainly see that life in Yi Dynasty Korea was very similar to life in North Korea today.

識字率と平均寿命を別にすれば、李氏朝鮮の生活は、大まかに言って今の北朝鮮の生活に極めて近いことがよく分かります。

Compare this to Japan. When American Commodore Perry arrived in Japan in 1853 to force Japan to trade with America, literacy rate among the general population in America was 40%, in Japan 80%.

これを日本と比べてみましょう。1853年に、アメリカのペリー提督が日本にアメリカとの交易を強要するために日本に来た時、アメリカ人の識字率は40％、一方日本人の識字率は80％でした。

It was not until the annexation by Japan that the use of Hangul spread throughout Korean society, and that education for the masses was developed.

朝鮮全域でハングルが広く使用されるようになり、一般庶民への教育が広まったのは、日本が朝鮮を併合してからのことでした。

Confucianism is a strictly hierarchical system, and this was rooted in the Korean society of the time. There was little entertainment for the common people, and no great culture. There were folk dances and such to be sure, but there was little in the way of inspirational art developed by commoners. Innovation was strictly repressed.

儒教は厳しい階層的なシステムで、当時の李氏朝鮮の社会に根付いていました。一般庶民のための娯楽はほとんどなく、優れた文化もありません。フォークダンスのようなものは確かにありましたが、庶民が作った感化的芸術のようなものはありませんでした。革新的なものは厳しく抑えられました。

I think that the Yangban looked down upon such things as being possibly revolutionary in nature. In fact, the Yi dynasty Korean military was meant to be mainly a force to keep internal order. That is why when called upon to fight a foreign invader, they usually did poorly.

両班はそういう芸術や文化的なものを、大変革をもたらし兼ねない性格のことして見下していたのだと考えます。実は、李氏朝鮮軍は、国内の秩序を維持するために存在していました。そのため、外国から侵略された場合、ほとんど役に立ちませんでした。

The Nobles who ruined the country
国を滅ぼした両班

Intrigue among the noble classes was also debilitating to the nation. For example, in the Imjin War, the Korean armies did very poorly against the invading Japanese forces. But one General did have great military ability, and was praised by Japanese Baron Konishi Yukinaga. His name was Kim. What was his reward for such success against Japanese forces? He was executed by jealous officials.

両班の策謀は国を衰退させました。たとえば、秀吉の朝鮮出兵の時、侵攻する日本軍に、李氏朝鮮軍はほとんど勝てませんでした。しかし李氏朝鮮に軍事的な才能がある将軍が一人いました。小西行長が彼を称賛しています。その将軍は、金将軍。しかし、日本軍との戦いで活躍した彼の報酬は何だったでしょうか？ 彼は、嫉妬深い官吏に処刑されたのでした。

Koreans think that Admiral Yi Sun-shin of the Yi dynasty Korean Navy deserved a lot of credit for forcing Japanese forces to abandon the Korean invasion. It follows that his turtle ships, and iron-clad warships, and novel naval tactics could be said to have saved the nation. Well, since at the time, Japan did not have a formal Navy, the seaborne part of Toyotomi's invasion was left to pirate Barons to handle. Yet Yi Sun-shin's reward was demotion to a common seaman, after he barely escaped execution.

日本軍を朝鮮侵略の断念に追い込んだ李氏朝鮮水軍の李舜臣将軍の功績は大きかったと韓国人は考えています。彼の亀甲船、装甲軍艦、および新奇な海上作戦が国を救ったと言えなくもないという訳です。ところで、当時日本には正規の水軍がなかったので、豊臣秀吉による朝鮮出兵での海上輸送は海賊大名に任せられました。しかし、李舜臣への報いは、辛うじて死刑を免れた後、将軍から兵卒への降格でした。

And corruption was omnipresent, to the point that the Korean justice system functioned only for the highest briber.

そして、腐敗がはびこり、李氏朝鮮における司法制度の恩恵に与れるのは最高値の賄賂を支払う者だけという有様でした。

As we shall see, this intrigue among officials was one of the reasons Japan annexed Korea outright. Japan could not put trust in whether Yi dynasty Korea would lean towards Russia or Japan, and so was ill at ease. Such constant intrigue produced a government that was basically incompetent.

後述するが、このような両班の策謀が、日本が朝鮮を公然と併合した大きな理由の一つです。李氏朝鮮は日本側につくのか、ロシア側につくのか、日本は信用できず不安でした。そのような両班の策謀が常にあったため、李氏朝鮮の政府は無能でした。

And such strict adherence to Confucianist philosophy produced a nation with no artistic innovation, and all artistic expression was frozen into an unchanging steady state form.

そして、儒教の教えに固執していたため、芸術が革新されることがない国となり、あらゆる芸術的表現が凍結され、旧態依然としたままでした。

Even the Korean Kings themselves had to have approval by the Chinese Emperor. Whenever a new King was crowned, the Chinese Emperor would send an emissary. The emissary would arrive at the Yeongeunmun Gate, Seoul, and read an official document from the Emperor of China approving of the new Korean King. The Korean King would go on his knees and bow his face into the dirt before the emissary from China.

李氏朝鮮は国王が即位する時、中国の皇帝からの承認が必要でした。新しい国王が戴冠する時には、中国の皇帝が勅使を送ります。勅使はソウルの迎恩門に着くと、新国王を承認する中国皇帝からの文書を読みます。李氏朝鮮の国王は、中国の勅使の前に膝まずいて、頭を地面に付けます。

Yi dynasty Korea was a complete vassal state of China both politically and socially. Japan, while having commerce with China, made no such submission. Thus, the Koreans looked down upon Japan as barbarians, and considered themselves superior.

　李氏朝鮮は、政治的にも社会的にも、完全に中国の属国でした。日本は中国と貿易していましたが、服従関係にはありませんでした。それで、李氏朝鮮時代の朝鮮人は、日本は野蛮人の国だと見下し、自分たちは日本より上位の国であると思っていました。

Yeongeunmun Gate. This was the gate where the Korean King performed the courtesy of three kneelings and nine kowtows to the Chinese emperor's emissary. After Japan's victory in the Sino-Japanese War, and Korea's separation from China's tributary system, it was torn down, and on the site is now the Independence Gate.

迎恩門。朝鮮の歴代の王はここで、中国皇帝の勅使を三跪九叩頭《さんききゅうこうとう》の礼で迎えた。日清戦争で日本が勝利し、朝鮮が清の冊封体制から離脱すると、迎恩門は取り壊され、独立門が建てられた。

Vibrant Edo era as contrasted with Yi dynasty Korea
李氏朝鮮と対照的だった活気ある江戸時代

Japan, on the other hand, flowered in culture in the Edo era. To the Westerner, it may seem to be a contradiction. The Tokugawa government was a military government that did not wage war. It was ruled by the Tokugawa clan. To be sure, there were enemy clans, most notably the Shimazu and Mori clans.

逆に、江戸時代に日本の文化は栄えました。西洋人は、そんなはずはないと思うかもしれません。徳川幕府は、戦争を行わない軍事政権でした。幕府は徳川家が支配しました。確かに、敵対的な藩、たとえば、島津藩や毛利藩はいました。

But they were kept under control by various institutional checks set up by the Tokugawa government using political tactics. There was of course political intrigue and corruption to an extent, but they did not go so far as to interfere with the administration of the country.

しかし、徳川幕府は上手に政治力を使い、行動を起こさせないための様々な制度を作り、その敵対的な藩をコントロールしました。もちろん陰謀や腐敗はある程度ありましたが、国の運営を妨げるほどのものではありませんでした。

Edo, Osaka and other cities in Japan were clean cities. There was a well-organized water supply and sewerage system, with underground wooden channels, and on top of it a waste disposal system, which treated garbage and human waste. This was different from Korea, where they were simply thrown on the street in those days, creating a malodorous environment, and making deadly diseases endemic.

江戸、大坂、その他の日本の街は、どこも綺麗でした。特に江戸には上下水道ができていて、街中に木製の配管がめぐらされていました。そして、ゴミや糞尿を処理するシステムもありました。これは、李氏朝鮮とは全然違います。当時の朝鮮では、ゴミも糞尿もそのまま通りに捨てられていました。悪臭を放つひどい環境で、危険な風土病が蔓延していました。

And in Japan, during this Edo period, literacy rate was about 80% of population, while in Yi dynasty Korea only a tiny minority of the upper class could read and write.

それから、日本では、江戸時代の識字率は人口の８割でしたが、李氏朝鮮では、文字を読める人は一番上の階級でも少数でした。

The Edo era saw an extreme explosion of artistic creativity. Noh was for the noble classes, but for the common people Kabuki became very popular. Ukiyoe woodblock prints entertained people, along with their erotic form, Shunga. Sumo wrestling enjoyed popularity as a national sport.

江戸時代は、芸術の創造性が爆発的に発展しました。能楽は貴族・武士階級に好まれ、平民の間では歌舞伎が大人気となりました。浮世絵も性的表現の春画も、人々を楽しませる娯楽として発展し、大相撲も国民的娯楽として人気を博しました。

There were no equivalent to these entertainments in Yi dynasty Korea, and modern-day Koreans are jealous of this.

李氏朝鮮には、このような庶民も楽しめる娯楽は全くありませんでした。現在の韓国人はこのことをとても嫉妬しています。

The true reasons for the annexation of Korea
朝鮮併合の真因

There were many factors which acted in the annexation of Korea by Japan. Basically, we can sum them up as strong Japanese will and efforts to survive, and Yi dynasty Korean utter incompetence.

日本の朝鮮併合にはいくつもの要因がありました。基本的に、日本には独立国として生き残ろうとする強い意志と努力があったのに対し、李氏朝鮮は全く無能であったと総括できます。

What do I mean by incompetence? Well, the arrival of Western powers carving out colonial empires in Asia was like a massive earthquake. China was weak and could not resist. Yi dynasty Korea chose to ignore things and maintain its isolation.

無能というのはどういう意味でしょうか？ そうですね、植民地帝国を切り出す欧米列強のアジアへの到来は、まるで大地震のような衝撃をもたらしました。清は弱くて、対抗できませんでした。李氏朝鮮はこの事態を無視し孤立する道を選んだのです。

In Japan, a coalition led by the Mori and Shimazu fiefs made a Meiji Restoration and paved the way for modernizing the country. Everywhere Japan looked predatory Western powers were lurking with a keen eye.

　日本では、毛利藩と島津藩を中心とした連合が明治維新を起こして、日本を近代国家へと導きました。日本の周りでは略奪的な欧米列強が虎視眈々と狙っているように見えました。

Yi dynasty Korea was roiled by internal disorder. But unlike Japan, there was no capable force like the Western Barons, Mori and Shimazu to oppose the government. The revolutionaries in Korea were basically peasant armies. Since the Yi dynasty Korean peasantry was illiterate, and with no experience of leadership, they could not organize effectively.

　李氏朝鮮は内患のため混乱するばかりでした。李氏朝鮮には、日本と違って西国の雄毛利藩や島津藩のような政体に反抗できる有能な力がありませんでした。李氏朝鮮の革命軍は基本的に農民の軍でした。李氏朝鮮の農民は読み書きができず、統率する経験もなかったので、効率的に結束することができませんでした。

Also, the Yi dynasty Korean government forces, suffering from neglect and corruption, could not put the rebellions down, and chaos roiled the country.

　その上、政府の怠慢と腐敗に病む李氏朝鮮の政府軍は、反乱を鎮圧できず、国が大混乱になりました。

The First Sino-Japanese War
日清戦争

Let's look at a war between China and Japan.

それでは日清戦争について見てみましょう。

In 1894 China sent troops into Korea at the request of the Yi dynasty Korean King.

1894年、清国は李氏朝鮮の王からの要請により陸軍の部隊を朝鮮に派遣しました。

The result was a war in which Japan soundly beat China. Despite the Chinese Navy possessing the most modern warships built in European yards, lack of control due to lack of training doomed the Chinese effort. As a matter of course, China lost.

日本と清の間で戦争になりましたが、結果は日本の圧勝でした。清国海軍はヨーロッパで造られた最新の軍艦を持っていましたが、訓練不足で統率がとれておらず、中国の努力を無に帰しました。当然中国が敗北しました。

As part of the peace treaty, Japan occupied the strategic Liaodong Peninsula. It was at this juncture that Russia, Germany and France stepped in. They put diplomatic pressure on Japan to give up the Liaodong Peninsula to China. Those white countries were very condescending to Japan, saying that this sort of thing was not how a civilized country conducted itself.

講和条約の一つの条件に、日本は戦略的に重要な遼東半島の割譲を受けました。ロシア、ドイツ、フランスの三ヵ国が介入したのはこの時でした。三国は、遼東半島を清に返還するよう日本に外交的圧力をかけました。それらの白人国家は日本に対して、非常に見下したように、文明国はそのようなことをしないと言いました。

It was soon after that that Russia moved into the Liaodong Peninsula and built a major naval base at Port Arthur.

その後すぐにロシアが遼東半島に入り、旅順に大きな海軍基地を置きました。

There is a thing I keep experiencing while talking with Westerners. They keep saying that Japan should have stayed within her own islands. They also say that the First Sino-Japanese War was the beginning of Japanese policy of aggression. This is particularly true of Americans.

西洋人といると､何度も経験することがあります。彼らは、日本は自分の島に留まっておくべきで、日清戦争は日本の侵略政策の始まりだったと言います。アメリカ人は特にそう言います。

But they ignore the fact that their countries, America included, were colonizing various parts and expanding their empires by force all throughout Asia and the world. Well, how could Japan be bad by simply trying to survive? These same Westerners say that Japan should have depended upon Western powers for food, fuel, and steel, essential things for a modern nation.

しかし、欧米人は、アメリカを含め西洋人諸国が世界各地を武力で植民地にして、帝国を拡げていた事実を無視しています。日本が生存のためにしたことがどうして悪なのでしょうか？ 同じ欧米人が、日本は食料、燃料、鉄といった近代的な国家に必須な資源を、欧米諸国に頼ればよかった、と言います。

But are Western countries truly benevolent? The truth of history shows us differently. Japan faces the same problem with the TPP treaty today. It is simply another form of colonial control, this time by American corporations, not by the American government. The conversation is simply another form of Western hate against Japan. What they mean is that Japan is an inferior country, and so Japan should never be allowed status equal to that of Western countries. This feeling continues today.

Chinese battleship Dingyuan. She was scuttled to avoid capture after being damaged by a Japanese torpedo and shellfire. Built to order in Germany together with her sister ship Zhenyuan, at the time she was called the most powerful warship in the East.

清国海軍の戦艦定遠。日本海軍の魚雷と砲撃で損傷を受け、鹵獲を避けるため自沈。同型艦の鎮遠とともにドイツに発注、建造された戦艦で、当時東洋一の堅艦と呼ばれた。

しかし、欧米列強はそんなに親切な国なのでしょうか？歴史を見ると、全然違うことが分かります。現在、日本はTPPの条約で同じ問題に直面しています。この条約は、形を変えた植民地支配です。今回はアメリカ政府ではなく、アメリカの企業です。先の会話は、西洋人の日本に対する単なる別の形でのヘイトです。彼らは、日本が西洋より劣った国であり、日本が西洋と対等な立場に立つことを絶対に許さない、と言っているのです。この感覚は今も変わりません。

The end stage of the Yi dynasty Korea
末期状態だった李氏朝鮮

After the First Sino-Japanese War, Japan tried to help Yi dynasty Korea stand up as an independent country. It proved to be impossible. There were no trained technocrats in the country at all. In the Meiji period, Japan sent people to Europe and America to be trained in skills to manage modern technology in all fields, all to develop Japan into a modern nation.

日清戦争後、日本が李氏朝鮮を独立国として立ち上がるよう援助しましたが、それは不可能でした。李氏朝鮮には専門的な技術官僚が一人もいなかったのです。明治時代には、日本は、近代国家へと発展するために、欧米から様々な分野の最新の技術を学ぶために人材を派遣しました。

In Yi dynasty Korea, nothing of the sort was done. In fact, the Korean court was always playing games of intrigue between Japan and Russia. The Yi dynasty Korean King even fled to the Russian legation for protection and stayed there for one year during one of the many revolts of this period.

李氏朝鮮は、そんな行動を全く行いませんでした。実際に、李氏宮廷は日本とロシアの間でいつまでも策謀ゲームを行っていました。この期間、頻発した反乱の一つの折に、李氏朝鮮の国王は自分の命を守るためにロシア公使館に逃げ1年間隠れました。

There were Korean activists who wanted to westernize their country, and survive as a Korean nation. One of the most notable was Kim Ok Gyun. He formed an independence party with like-minded Yangban. He also admired Japan for its successful Meiji Restoration, and studied at Japan's Keio university under the sponsorship of Fukuzawa Yukichi, to aim to modernize Korea on Japan model.

当時朝鮮を西洋化して、朝鮮の独立を守りたいと考える活動家がいました。有名な人物に、金玉均がいます。彼は同じ志を持つ両班と共に独立党を作りました。彼は、日本の明治維新の成功を称賛し、これを模範として朝鮮の近代化を目指し、福澤諭吉の支援を受け、慶応義塾で学びました。

Eventually, he made a successful coup in Seoul, but the plan had been betrayed to the Queen, who called to the Chinese Army for help. The coup members fled to Japan.

結局、彼はソウルでクーデターをうまく起こしましたが、秘密が皇后に漏れていたため、皇后は清軍に助けを求めてしまいました。クーデターを実行したメンバーは日本へ逃れました。

In 1893, while on route to Shanghai from Japan to visit another revolutionary, Kim Ok Gyun was assassinated. His body was sent to Korea, where it was dismembered, and the various body parts put on public display in various towns throughout the nation.

1893年、他の革命家と会うため、日本から上海への途上、金玉均は暗殺されました。彼の死体は朝鮮へ送られ、そこでバラバラに切断され、死体の各部が国中の様々な街で晒されました。

Kim Ok Gyun, late Yi dynasty Korean revolutionary and leader for Korea's independence. He aimed for Korea's independence from China and modernization on the level of the Meiji Revolution. He fled to Japan as a refugee after an attempted coup. After that, he was assassinated in Shanghai. His dismembered body was displayed throughout Korea.

金玉均。李氏朝鮮後期の革命家で朝鮮独立の指導者。明治維新を模範として清からの独立と朝鮮近代化を目指したが、クーデターに失敗して日本に亡命。その後上海で暗殺され、バラバラにされた遺体は朝鮮各地で晒された。

The Russo-Japanese War
日露戦争

The Russo-Japanese War resulted from continued encroachments by Russia into Korea. Russian companies operated in Korea. But they secretly were constructing Naval bases. One was to be located at Masan, near the present city of Pusan, and not so far from Tsushima.

日露戦争の原因は、ロシアによる朝鮮への連続した侵略です。ロシアの会社が朝鮮内で活動していました。しかし、実は密かにロシアの海軍基地を造っていました。その海軍基地の計画の一つは馬山で、現在の釜山市の近く、対馬の目と鼻の先でした。

This was intolerable to Japan, and the Russo-Japanese War, which was an overwhelming victory for Japan, resulted.

日本はそんなことを許容できず、日本の圧倒的勝利となった日露戦争が起こりました。

While the Russian soldiers and sailors fought much more bravely than Chinese or Korean troops, their leadership was completely incompetent. Their only decent military leader was admiral Makarov, who energetically led the Russian fleet at Port Arthur.

清軍や朝鮮軍に比べ、ロシアの陸海軍兵士ははるかに勇敢に戦いましたが、ロシアの指導部はほとんど役に立ちませんでした。唯一まともなロシアの軍事指揮官は、海軍のマカロフ提督で、旅順港のロシア艦隊を強力に統率しました。

He had 7 battleships there to Japan's 6, and he could have made things very difficult for Japan. But his flagship struck a mine laid by the Japanese navy while returning to Port Arthur after a naval battle with the Japanese fleet, and sank within minutes. The next commander of the Russian Pacific fleet remained in Port Arthur, declining to engage the Japanese fleet in combat.

日本の戦艦６隻に対し、旅順港のロシア艦隊は戦艦７隻でした。マカロフ提督は、日本にとって非常にやっかいな存在でした。しかし、彼が座乗する旗艦は、日本艦隊との海戦の後、旅順に帰投する時に日本軍の敷設した機雷に接触し、数分で沈没しました。次のロシア太平洋艦隊の司令官は、旅順港にこもって、日本艦隊を海戦に誘うことを避けていました。

Japan won the war overwhelmingly.

日本は日露戦争で大勝利をおさめました。

Admiral Stepan Makarov, one of the great officers of the Imperial Russian Navy and a master of naval tactics. He was the first in the world to launch a torpedo attack against the Turkish fleet, and he developed the basic concept of torpedo warfare.

ロシア帝国海軍提督の一人ステファン・マカロフ。海軍戦術論の大家で、オスマン帝国のトルコ艦隊に対して世界初の雷撃を敢行、魚雷戦の基本理論を考案した。

Chapter 5
The truth of the annexation period
併合時代の真実

Examining documents of the annexation period
併合当時の資料を読む

Japan decided therefore that outright annexation and direct rule was the only possible solution. Again, many Westerners insist that it was a brutal occupation. Very fortunately, we have some observations by a professional observer, Mr. Alleyne Ireland. He was British. He was appointed by the University of Chicago as a Commissioner in charge of colonial administration, and sent to the Far East to study American, Japanese, Dutch, British, and French Colonial systems.

そのため日本は、完全な併合と直接統治が唯一の可能な解決策だと判断しました。繰り返しますが、欧米人の多くは、それは残酷な占領だったと主張します。非常に幸運なことに、プロの観察者であるアレン・アイルランド氏による見解があります。彼はイギリス人でした。彼はシカゴ大学から植民地行政担当委員に任命され、極東に派遣されてアメリカ、日本、オランダ、イギリス、フランスの植民地制度を研究しました。

The following statistics that I use are all from his book “The New Korea”. He visited Korea in 1922, and published his book in 1926.

以下の統計はすべて、彼の著書『The New Korea』から引用したものです。彼は1922年に朝鮮を訪れ、1926年に本を出版しました。

I truly think that to describe the Japanese annexation of Korea, we should use the word "uplift". With colonialism, it was purely exploitive. The motive for acquiring rule over another country was simply profit.

　私は、日本の朝鮮併合を表現するには、「高揚」「向上」という言葉を使うべきだと心から思います。植民地主義は純粋に搾取的でした。他国の支配権を獲得する動機は単に利益でした。

Investment in that country was therefore kept to a minimum. Schools, hospitals, railroads, were only built to further profit. Japan was different. When Commodore Perry came to Japan in 1853, Japanese were awestruck by American military technology.

　そのため、同国への投資は最小限に抑えられました。学校も病院も鉄道も、利益を上げるためだけに建設されました。日本は違いました。1853年にペリー提督が来日したとき、日本人はアメリカの軍事技術に驚愕しました。

People very quickly realized that if Japan did not adopt such modern technology itself, Japan, would come under the domination and rule of the Americans or other Westerners.

　もし日本が自らそのような近代技術を採用しなければ、日本はアメリカ人やその他の西洋人の支配下に置かれることになると、人々はすぐに気づきました。

So Japan sent many young men to Europe and the United States to acquire this new technical knowledge. Yet Japan did not give up her culture and language to the West, but preserved it. In fact, many Westerners came to admire Japanese literature, Kabuki, and other cultural traditions.

そこで日本は多くの若者を欧米に送り込み、この新しい技術的知識を習得させました。しかし、日本は文化や言語を西洋に譲ったのではなく、守り通しました。実際、多くの西洋人が日本の文学や歌舞伎、その他の文化的伝統を賞賛するようになりました。

In the Edo era, Japan had 264 years of peace, in which cultural development flourished, all under a military government.

江戸時代の日本は264年間平和で、文化的発展が花開きました。

Korea had no such cultural growth. The Joseon dynasty, founded in 1392, did not allow cultural development. It was a society designed to preserve the ruling order. Education of the masses was not provided, in fact, 40% to 60% of Koreans were slaves. Estimates vary. Sanitation was poor, and life spans were short.

李氏朝鮮にはそのような文化的発展はありませんでした。1392年に建国された李氏朝鮮は、文化の発展を許しませんでした。朝鮮李氏王朝は支配秩序を維持するための社会でした。大衆の教育は提供されず、事実、朝鮮人の40%から

60％は奴隷でした。推定はさまざまです。衛生状態は悪く、寿命は短かったです。

There was little to no cultural life for the common people, unlike Japan, no literature was produced which has enthralled the world.

日本とは異なり、庶民の文化的生活はほとんどなく、世界を魅了するような文学も生まれませんでした。

This is the Korea that Japan found upon annexation. Both countries had retreated into isolation before the arrival of Westerners. But Japan by embracing the technology of the West while maintaining her own culture, emerged as a vibrant country. Upon the coming of Western powers to North Asia, Korea retreated farther into isolation.

これが、日本が併合時に発見した朝鮮です。どちらの国も、西洋人がやってくるまでは鎖国をしていました。しかし、日本は、自国の文化を維持しながら西洋の技術を取り入れることで、活気ある国として浮上しました。西洋列強が北アジアにやってくると、朝鮮はさらに孤立していきました。

After the first Sino-Japanese war, Japanese officials were appointed as counsellors by the Korean King to administer the country. This idea was put forth by Japan. The problem was that the Yi dynasty Korean government had not sent any Koreans to be trained in the West in modern techniques of government, and therefore there were no Koreans educated in the field.

日清戦争の後、日本の役人が朝鮮国王の参事官に任命されました。これは日本が打ち出したアイデアでした。問題は、李氏朝鮮政府が朝鮮人を西洋に派遣して近代的な統治技術を学ばせていなかったため、その分野で教育を受けた朝鮮人がいなかったことです。

Also, Korean officials were very corrupt. Particularly in the case of magistrates, Japanese magistrates were quite popular, as they could not be bribed.

また、李氏朝鮮の役人は非常に腐敗していました。特に奉行の場合、日本の奉行は賄賂をもらえないので、かなり人気がありました。

After the annexation, even though Japan ruled Korea directly, every effort was made so that Koreans would be trained in modern government, and promoted through the ranks.

併合後、日本が朝鮮を直接統治していたとはいえ、朝鮮人が近代的な政治を学び、昇進できるようあらゆる努力が払われました。

Unlike other Western colonial powers, Japan embarked upon a course to raise Korea up to Japan's own level of cultural and technological development. This is in fact unique in world history, and why I call it "uplift".

他の西洋の植民地支配国とは異なり、日本は李氏朝鮮を日本の文化的・技術的発展の水準まで引き上げるという路線に乗り出しました。これは事実、世界史上類を見ないことであり、私がこれを「引き上げ」と呼ぶ所以です。

In fact, in the English language, uplift does not have this meaning, to raise up a more primitive culture to one's own, it means to cheer another person up. Westerners would just not understand the raising up of someone without self profit.

実際、英語では“uplift ”には、より原始的な文化を自分の文化に引き上げるという意味はなく、他人を元気づけるという意味があります。欧米人には、私利私欲のない人を引き上げるということが理解出来ません。

A view of Seoul before and after annexation.

日本統治前と後のソウル。

Local government was completely built up from scratch.

地方政府は完全にゼロから作り上げられました。

On the provincial level, for budget purposes, five departments were created; Public Works, Sanitation and Hospitals, Relief and Charity, Industrial encouragement, and Education.

地方政府レベルでは、予算編成のため、公共事業、衛生・病院、救済・慈善、産業奨励、教育の５部門が設けられました。

No such organizations existed in Yi dynasty Korea. These organizations promoted the welfare of the Korean people. For example, the Koreans often say that the mountains are bare of trees because Japan cut down all the trees during their rule. The opposite is true. The forests had been destroyed by corrupt Yi dynasty officials. Under the above Industrial encouragement, forestry seedling stations were established at the local level throughout the Korean Peninsula.

李氏朝鮮にはこのような組織は存在しませんでした。これらの組織は朝鮮の人々の福祉を促進しました。例えば、韓国人はよく「日本が併合時代に木を切り倒したから、山には木がない」と言います。その逆です。森林は腐敗した李朝官吏によって破壊されました。以上のような産業奨励のもと、朝鮮半島各地に林業苗木ステーションが設置されました。

A legal system created from primitive beginnings.
原始的な始まりから生まれた法制度

In Yi dynasty Korea, law was administered by royal court appointed officials. They were all corrupt, and favorable verdicts were handed out to the highest bidder. Torture was commonly used, both on suspects who did not give a bribe and on witnesses. This was to gain testimony favoring the desired verdict.

李氏朝鮮では、法律は王室が任命した官吏によって管理されていました。彼らはみな腐敗しており、有利な判決は最高入札者に下されました。賄賂を渡さなかった容疑者にも、証人にも、拷問がよく行われました。これは、希望する判決に有利な証言を得るためでした。

There was no legal system built upon modern methods of the age.

この時代には、近代的な手法に基づいた法制度は存在しませんでした。

After annexation, in general, Japanese law became the law of the land. Japan had created a modern jurisprudence based upon legal systems as they had evolved in Europe and the United States. An exception was made for the crime of murder. Korean penalties were kept in this case. This was because the punishments for murder mandated by Japanese law were considered too mild to have an effect on Korean crimes. At this time murder cases were quite common in Korea.

併合後、一般的には日本法が国法となりました。日本は、欧米で発展してきた法制度に基づいた近代的な法学を作り上げました。ただし、殺人罪は例外でした。この場合、李氏朝鮮の刑罰が維持されました。日本の法律で定められた殺人罪は、李氏朝鮮時代の犯罪に影響を及ぼすには軽すぎると考えられたからです。この当時、李氏朝鮮では殺人事件がかなり頻発していました。

Flogging was amended so that women, children and the mentally disabled could not be punished by it. It was banned altogether in 1920.

鞭打ちが改正され、女性、子供、知的障害者は鞭打ちによる処罰を受けられなくなりました。1920 年には完全に禁止されました。

In Yi dynasty Korea there was no set court system. Often corrupt local police stations conducted trials and punishments on their own.

李氏朝鮮には決まった裁判制度がありませんでした。多くの場合、腐敗した地方警察署が独自に裁判や処罰を行っていました。

Under Japanese rule this was abolished, and by 1909 there were one Supreme court, 3 courts of appeal, 8 local courts, and 9 branch local courts, and 80 local courts.

日本統治下ではこれが廃止され、1909 年までに最高裁判所が１つ、控訴裁判所が３つ、地方裁判所が８つ、支部の地方裁判所が９つ、地方裁判所が 80 になりました。

In 1923 there were 162 Japanese and 37 Korean judges, 67 Japanese and 10 Korean public prosecutors, and 423 Japanese 232 Korean clerks and assistant interpreters.

1923年には、日本人裁判官162人、朝鮮人裁判官37人、日本人検察官67人、朝鮮人検察官10人、日本人書記官・通訳助手423人、朝鮮人書記官・通訳助手232人でした。

When one considers that before Japanese involvement in the internal affairs of Korea before Sino-Japanese War 1894 the number of Koreans who had an education qualifying themselves in modern legal affairs was zero, this was quire an accomplishment in 29 years.

1894年の日清戦争以前、日本が朝鮮の内政に関与する以前は、近代的な法律事務の資格を得る教育を受けた朝鮮人の数はゼロであったことを考えると、これは29年ぶりの快挙です。

The number of courts had expanded by 1925 to 1 Supreme Court, 3 Courts of appeal, 11 local courts, 46 branch local courts, 160 local courts.

1925年までに裁判所の数は拡大し、最高裁判所1、控訴裁判所3、地方裁判所11、支部地方裁判所46、地方裁判所160となりました。

And corruption, bribery, was non existent.

汚職や賄賂も存在しませんでした。

A police force built out thin air
何もないところから作られた警察組織

In Yi dynasty Korea, police functions were carried out by military garrisons throughout the country. There was no independent professional police force. In general, the garrisons abused the local population, and acted in the interest of rich and powerful people.

李氏朝鮮では、警察機能は全国各地の軍事駐屯地が担っていました。独立したプロの警察は存在しませんでした。一般的に、駐屯地は地元住民を虐待し、金持ちや権力者の利益のために行動しました。

In 1894 Japan created a police force separate from the military, and established a school in Seoul to train police officials. This did not prove sufficient to create an independent professional police force however.

1894年、日本は軍隊とは別に警察を創設し、警察官を養成するための学校をソウルに設立しました。しかし、これは独立した職業警察を創設するには十分ではありませんでした。

Thus in 1904 a large number of Japanese police were brought in to introduce professionalism in the ranks. In 1909 there were 36 Japanese and 11 Korean inspectors, 156 Japanese and 102 Korean sergeants, 1,1924 Japanese and 57 Korean interpreters, 63 Japanese physicians.

こうして1904年、階級にプロフェッショナリズムを導入するために、多数の日本人警察が導入されました。1909年には、日本人36人、朝鮮人11人の警視、日本人156人、朝鮮人102人の巡査部長、日本人11924人、朝鮮人57人の通訳、63人の日本人医師がいました。

There are many museums in Korea, with plaster mannequins showing the torture of Korean people by Japanese soldiers. The first counter argument to this is that Japanese soldiers basically did not interfere in day to day affairs in Korea. The second counter argument is that throughout the annexation, most rank and file police in Korea were ethnic Koreans.

韓国には多くの博物館があり、日本兵による朝鮮人拷問を示す石膏像が展示されています。これに対する第一の反論は、日本兵は基本的に朝鮮の日常業務には干渉しなかったというものです。第二の反論は、併合期間中、朝鮮の階級警察のほとんどは朝鮮民族だったということです。

If such torture had existed, Mr. Ireland would have certainly mentioned it, as he was a neutral observer. Instead, he noted that Yi dynasty Korean punishments were much much harsher than under Japanese rule.

もしそのような拷問があったなら、中立の立場で観察していたアイルランド氏は必ず言及しただろう。その代わりに彼は、李氏朝鮮時代の刑罰は日本統治下よりもはるかに厳しかったと指摘しました。

And this is part of the reason for Korea screaming about Japan today. They know themselves in their hearts, but they truly don' t understand Japan. Thus they ascribe the more terrible aspects of the Korean soul to Japan.

そしてこれが、韓国が今日、日本に対して悲鳴を上げている理由の一部です。彼らは心の中では自分たちのことを知っているが、本当に日本を理解していません。こうして彼らは、韓国人の魂のより恐ろしい側面を日本に当てはめてしまうのです。

Between the Sino Japanese war and the annexation, a gendarme force was created to deal with bandits. All throughout Korean history there were marauding gangs of bandits throughout the country. By 1909, there were 2,369 Japanese and 4,392 Koreans stationed at 499 posts of the gendarmerie in peninsula.

日清戦争から併合までの間に、匪賊に対処するための憲兵隊が創設された。朝鮮の歴史を通じて、国中に匪賊の襲撃団がいた。1909 年まで、半島の憲兵隊 499 カ所に日本人 2,369 人と朝鮮人 4,392 人が駐屯していました。

In 1922 the number of police was 1,161 Japanese 422 Korean officers, and 11,028 Japanese 8,160 Korean policemen in Korea. The total population was 17 million.

1922 年の警察官の数は、日本人 1,161 人、朝鮮人 422 人、日本人 11,028 人、朝鮮人 8,160 人でした。総人口は 1700 万人でした。

Conditions in Yi dynasty prisons were terrible for prisoners.

They were very overcrowded. When Japan took over, it was found that the average prisoner had only 5 square feet of space. Japan reformed the system totally, and Mr. Ireland stated that Japanese run prisons were better than most American prisons of the day.

李朝の刑務所の状況は、囚人にとってひどいものでした。非常に過密でした。日本が引き継いだとき、平均的な囚人のスペースはわずか5平方フィートしかないことが分かりました。日本はシステムを全面的に改革し、アイルランド氏は、日本の刑務所は当時のアメリカのほとんどの刑務所よりも優れていると述べました。

The death rate of prisoners was very low. In the five years ending in 1923, the average daily prison population was 15,220, and the average annual death rate was 288. The tales that Korean people tell of torture and murder by Japanese police in Korean prisons are simply myth.

囚人の死亡率は非常に低かったです。1923年までの5年間で、1日の平均囚人数は15,220人、年間平均死亡率は288人でした。韓国人が語る平吾時代の刑務所での日本警察による拷問や殺人の話は、単なる作り話です。

Replacing a chaotic financial system with order
混沌とした金融システムを秩序に置き換える

In Yi dynasty Korea, finances were chaotic to say the least. There were two financial departments of the Yi dynasty government, that of the State and that of the Royal household.

They were supposed to be independent of each other, but the Royal household often took funds from the State financial department.

李氏朝鮮時代の財政は、控えめに言っても混沌としていました。李朝政府には２つの財政部門があり、国の財政部門と王室の財政部門であります。両者は互いに独立しているはずだったが、王室はしばしば国家財政部から資金を調達していました。

There was much abuse and thievery that went with the collection of taxes. Rights to mint coinage which competed with the national were sold to the highest bidder. Thus it can be said that Yi dynasty Korea did not possess a trustworthy currency.

税金の徴収には多くの悪用と泥棒がありました。国家と競合する貨幣を鋳造する権利は、最も高い入札者に売られました。このように、李氏朝鮮は信頼できる通貨を持っていなかったと言えます。

As Japan took over administration of the country, land registration was clarified so as to provide a reliable tax base, a central bank was established along with a reliable currency, and these were all subsidized by loans from Japan.

日本が国の統治を引き継いだことで、土地登記が明確化され、確実な課税基盤となり、中央銀行が設立され、確実な通貨が供給されるようになりました。

Education
教育

The first formal Korean education system was begun in 1398 when the founderr of Yi dynasty, King Taejo (Yi Seong Gye) established a university in Seoul. Schools were also established in the provinces.

李氏朝鮮初の正式な教育制度は、1398 年に李王朝の始祖である太祖（李成桂）がソウルに大学を設立したときに始まりました。地方にも学校が設立されました。

The third Yi dynasty king, Taejong added preparatory schools. These schools were supported in their expenditures by the revenues of government farms where slaves worked. Instruction was given on Chinese Confucianism so that students could pass the examination for officials.

李朝第３代王の太宗は、予備学校を加えました。これらの学校の支出は、奴隷が働く官営農場の収入によって支えられました。生徒たちが官吏試験に合格できるよう、中国の儒教についての指導が行われました。

There were also privately run schools called Seodang which taught written Chinese.

また、中国語の筆記を教える書堂と呼ばれる私立の学校もありました。

There was no education in modern technical or scientific fields.

近代的な技術や科学分野の教育はありませんでした。

As long as Korea lived in isolation, this system which could only produce Confucian scholars, was good enough. But when Western powers began to encroach upon Asia, such scholars could not comprehend what was happening.

朝鮮が孤立して暮らしている間は、儒学者しか輩出できないこのシステムで十分でした。しかし、西洋列強がアジアを侵略し始めると、そのような学者たちは何が起こっているのか理解できなくなりました。

As Japan took over administration of the country, change was rapid. At first three things were done. One was to establish a school for girls. The Yi dynasty Korean government had not done anything in this area.

日本がこの国の統治を引き継ぐと、変化は急速でした。最初は3つのことが行われました。ひとつは女学校の設立でした。李氏朝鮮時代はこの分野で何もしていませんでした。

The second was the establishment of Commercial, Technical, and Agricultural schools. Baron Okura of Japan personally funded a private commercial school with a huge amount of money in 1906.

二つ目は、商業学校、技術学校、農業学校の設立です。日本の大倉男爵は 1906 年、私立の商業学校に個人的に巨額の資金を提供しました。

The third thing done was to place private schools under the supervision of the government. Before this time, there had been no attempt to control them. Standards of education varied widely, many were schools in name only, which existed only to make money and whose educational levels were quite low.

三つ目は、私立学校を政府の監督下に置くことでした。それまでは、私立学校を管理しようという試みはありませんでした。教育の水準は千差万別で、多くは名ばかりの学校で、金儲けのためだけに存在し、その教育レベルはかなり低かったです。

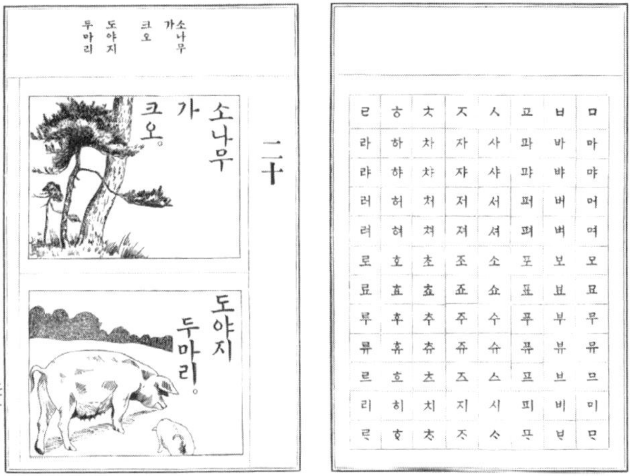

A Korean textbook in use during the annexation period. Notice that it teaches the Korean Hangul script.

日本統治時代に学校教育で使用された朝鮮語読本。朝鮮のハングル文字も教えていることに注目。

Standards were set and approved textbooks distributed.

基準が設定され、承認された教科書が配布されました。

As Japanese people came to settle in Korea, a dual system was set up. At first, Korean and Japanese children went to separate schools. this could not be helped, as the gap was too wide in education. As time went on, unified schools for both children who spoke mainly Korean, and those who spoke mainly Japanese were created. Children of either Korean or Japanese background could attend the school of their choice.

日本人が朝鮮に定住するようになると、二重制度が設けられました。当初、朝鮮人と日本人の子どもたちは別々の学校に通っていました。時が経つにつれ、朝鮮語を主に話す子供たちと日本語を主に話す子供たちのための統一学校が作られました。朝鮮系、日本系どちらの子どもたちも、希望する学校に通うことができるようになりました。

The fact is that many of the Japanese who settled in Korea learned to speak Korean.

事実、朝鮮に定住した日本人の多くは朝鮮語を話せるようになりました。

As far is Christianity is concerned, there was no discrimination. Schools that wished to have government verification, could not teach the Bible during school hours. But there was no prohibition of Bible study after regular school hours.

キリスト教に関する限り、差別はなかったです。政府の認可を受けたい学校は、授業時間中に聖書を教えることは出来ませんでした。しかし、正規の授業時間外に聖書を学ぶことは禁止されていませんでした。

There were sometimes Shinto religious ceremonies with students. Shinto was the State religion of Japan, and Korea had been annexed after all. However, Christian students could be excused from such ceremonies due to their beliefs.

神道は日本の国教であり、朝鮮はやはり併合されていました。神道は日本の国教であり、朝鮮は結局併合されたのです。しかし、クリスチャンの学生は、その信条からそのような儀式を免除されることもありました。

There are many people today who claim that Japan abolished the Korean writing system, Hangul, the phonetic alphabet. Not at all. Japan revived it.

今日、日本がハングルという表音文字を廃止したと主張する人がたくさんいます。そんなことはありません。日本はハングルを復活させたのです。

Hangul was first created in 1443 in the reign of King Sejong. It was later banned by King Yeonsangun. The reason was that the common people used Hangul to mock him.

ハングルは1443年、世宗《セジョン》王の時代に初めて作られました。その後、燕山君《ヨンサングン》王によって禁止されました。その理由は、庶民がハングルを使って世宗をあざむいたからです。

A new and modern Medical industry
新しく近代的な医療産業

In the Yi dynasty, medical services were performed by exorcists and shamans practicing folk medicine. No trained doctors existed in the country.

李朝時代、医療は民間療法を行う祓い師やシャーマンによって行われていました。訓練を受けた医師はこの国には存在しませんでした。

On the advice of Japan, the Korean government in 1897 issued instructions for vaccination against cholera, typhoid, diphtheria, and dysentery. However without professional doctors, the Korean government was unable to carry them out.

日本からの助言を受けて、1897年に朝鮮政府はコレラ、腸チフス、ジフテリア、赤痢に対する予防接種の指示を出しました。しかし、専門の医師がいなかったため、朝鮮政府はこれを実施することができませんでした。

Before the Japanese annexation, Korea did have a medical school, and a few Christian medical schools, but the equipment of these was very poor. So once annexation happened in 1910, the Japanese government built hospitals and made efforts to eradicate disease throughout the country.

日本が朝鮮を併合する前、朝鮮には医学校があり、キリスト教系の医学校もいくつかあったが、その設備は非常に貧弱でした。そのため、1910年に併合されると、日本政府は病院を建設し、朝鮮全土の病気の撲滅に努めました。

As we have seen, there was no custom of disposing of garbage and human waste, even in Seoul. Therefore, a mammoth effort had to be made to teach Korean people modern sanitary habits. The Japanese government also established facilities for producing clean drinking water.

これまで見てきたように、ソウルでさえゴミやし尿を処理する習慣がなかったです。そのため、朝鮮人に近代的な衛生習慣を教えるためには、膨大な努力が必要でした。日本政府もまた、清潔な飲料水を製造する施設を設立しました。

In this regard, a Central Health Agency, Hygienic Inspection Agency for inspecting the purity of food, beverages, and drugs, a Bacteriological Service for control of infectious diseases, and an Opium Control Office to fight Opium addiction, were all established.

この関連で、中央衛生局、食品・飲料・薬物の純度を検査する衛生検査局、伝染病を管理する細菌学サービス、アヘン中毒と闘うためのアヘン管理局が設立されました。

Government qualification standards were also established for doctors.

医師の資格基準も制定されました。

At the time of the annexation, the Imperial Japanese government also established a fund for disaster relief for Korean people. For example, a major drought occurred in 1919. Due to this fund, no one starved to death in Korea because of the drought.

併合当時、大日本帝国政府は朝鮮人に対する災害救済のための基金も設立しました。例えば、1919年に大干ばつが起きました。この基金のおかげで、朝鮮では干ばつによる餓死者は出ませんでした。

Agriculture

農業

During the Yi dynasty, land ownership was unclear, and agricultural techniques chaotic. In land ownership disputes, magistrates always ruled in favor of the richest party. The plight of Yi dynasty farmers, 80% of the population, was poor.

李朝時代、土地の所有権は不明確で、農業技術は混沌としていました。土地の所有権をめぐる争いでは、判官は常に富める者に有利な判決を下しました。人口の8割を占める李朝農民の苦境は貧しかったです。

In fact, most estimates give a figure of some 60% of the population being slaves. I think it can be assumed that most agricultural workers were slaves, under such a system, modern agricultural methods would not be developed.

実際、人口の60%が奴隷であったというのが大方の推測です。そのような体制では、近代的な農法は発達しなかったでしょう。

Japan established modern agricultural schools, and credit banks. The banks allowed farmers to purchase the land they worked by time payments, and improve agricultural implements.

日本は近代的な農業学校と信用銀行を設立しました。銀行は、農民が働いている土地を定期的に購入し、農具を改良することを可能にしました。

Since the average Korean farmer had difficulty in understanding the credit system, they could only comprehend it as another form of governmental thievery. Well, that was all they had known throughout their history. it took much time for them to understand the concepts of modern finance, banking, and

The Chosen Industrial Bank's main office. There were over 50 branches, providing uncollateralized loans to light industry and farmers.

朝鮮殖産銀行本店。50余の支店を有し、農工業者への無担保貸付を行った。

reliable currency.

平均的な朝鮮の農民は、信用システムを理解することが難しかったため、政府による泥棒の一形態としか理解できなかったです。彼らが近代的な金融、銀行、信頼できる通貨の概念を理解するには、かなりの時間を要しました。

To show the increase in agricultural production after annexation, we have the following figures. It is given in thousands of koku, 1 koku equals 5 bushels.

併合後の農業生産の増加を示すために、以下の数字があります。単位は千石で、1石は5ブッシェルに相当します。

	米（Rice）	大麦（Barley）	豆（Beans）
1912	10,865	5,856	4,733
1923	15,175	6,031	5,855

The improvement in agriculture is clear, which lead to an increase in the population.

農業の向上は明らかで、それが人口の増加につながりました。

The Japanese government selected superior varieties of rice from Japan, these included Wase-Shinriki from Kumamoto Prefecture, which could flourish even with little fertilizer, Kokuryo-Miyako from Yamaguchi Prefecture, well suited to making sake, and Tama-Nishiki from Tochigi Prefecture, which was very drought resistant.

日本政府は、肥料が少なくてもよく育つ熊本県産の「早生新力」、酒造りに適した山口県産の「国領都」、干ばつに強い栃木県産の「玉錦」など、日本から優れた品種を選抜しました。

The fishing industry did not exist except in some very local areas under the Yi dynasty. Fishing was developed as an industry throughout the peninsula under Japanese rule.

漁業は李朝時代にはごく一部の地域を除いて存在しなかったです。漁業は日本統治下の半島全域で産業として発展しました。

The city of Hungnam, an industrial jewel risen from the rice fields
田園から蘇った工業の宝石、興南の街

Japan created fertilizer and chemical plants in northeastern Korea at Hungnam, which had previously been rice fields. All throughout the northern section of the country, hydro- electric power generation was built. These plants also had their own facilities for machine production, one of them was the largest such plant in Korea.

日本は朝鮮北東部の興南《フンナム》に、それまで水田だった場所に肥料や化学製品の工場を作りました。朝鮮の北部一帯には水力発電所が建設されました。これらの工場には機械製造のための施設もあり、そのうちのひとつは朝鮮の最大の工場でした。

The Chosin reservoir dam, built to supply the complex with electricity, was the site of one of the US Marine Corps most famous battles in the Korean war.

複合施設に電力を供給するために建設された長津湖ダムは、朝鮮戦争における米海兵隊の最も有名な戦闘のひとつが行われた場所です。

Before the Japanese annexation Korea had basically been an agricultural country. These factories and power generation facilities built by Japan laid the basis for the industrial state South Korea is today.

日本が朝鮮を併合する前は、朝鮮は基本的に農業国でした。日本が建設した工場や発電施設は、今日の韓国の工業国家の基礎を築きました。

Although I may seem harsh on Korea, it is not my intention to insult Koreans. On the contrary, when I lived in South Korea, I found Koreans to be a very intelligent and hard working people. What I have presented here are simply facts. This is a partial explanation of how Japan and Korea interacted in the Western colonial era in Asia. If Korea had not been annexed by Japan, Some other Western country would have taken over Korea as a colonial dependency. The results of that domination would have been much crueler for Korea, and Korea would bear ill effects from rule even today. In fact, Koreans should have gratitude for the annexation. I ask Koreans to stop looking at this period with hysterical emotion, and examine the facts.

韓国に対して辛辣に見えるかもしれないが、韓国人を侮辱する意図はありません。それどころか、私が韓国に住んでいたとき、韓国人は非常に知的で勤勉な人々だと感じました。ここで紹介したことは、単なる事実です。これは、欧米のアジア植民地時代に日本と韓国がどのように交流していたかを部分的に説明したものである。もし韓国が日本に併合されていなかったら、西洋のどこかの国が植民地として韓国を支配していただろう。その支配の結果は韓国にとってもっと残酷なものであっただろうし、韓国は今日でも支配による弊害を背負っているだろう。実際、韓国人は併合に感謝すべきです。韓国人には、この時代をヒステリックな感情で見るのをやめて、事実を検証してほしいです。

Chapter 6
The present reality of Japanese-Korean relations
日韓問題の現実

The most peaceful and prosperous time in Korean history
韓国の歴史上最も平和で豊かだった時代

Was the Japanese annexation of Korea truly brutal, as many Western commentators state? They always use the word brutal, but they do not give any details.

多くの西洋人の解説者が言うように、日本の朝鮮併合は本当に残酷だったのでしょうか？ 彼らは、いつでも「残酷」という単語を使いますが、詳細は一切伝えません。

There was one violent demonstration during the Japanese annexation period. This was the March 1919 movement. Several hundred Koreans died in demonstrations across the country.

日本が併合している時代、1919年3月に荒れたデモが起きました。これは三・一運動のことです。朝鮮全域でのデモで、数百人の朝鮮人が死亡しました。

Until that time, Japanese Governor-Generals of Korea were former military men. After the demonstration, this was changed to civilians, and the type of government changed. For example, before the March 1919 movement, school teachers wore military uniforms and swords.

それ以前、朝鮮総督は元軍人でしたが、デモの後、総督武官制が廃止され、行政も変わりました。たとえば三・一運動の前には、学校の教員は軍服姿でサーベルを下げていました。

After that, this was abandoned by school teachers in favor of civilian dress. And thereafter there were no more riots of any great size, or demonstrations under Japanese rule. If the critics are correct in commenting even now that Japanese rule was brutal, Korea should have been seething with repeated revolutions.

その後、教員は旧習を止めて平服を着ました。それ以降、日本統治の間に大きな騒擾もデモも起こりませんでした。もし今も日本を批判している解説者の言うことが正しく日本の統治が本当に残酷なものだったのなら、当時の朝鮮は繰り返し革命が起きて騒然となっていたでしょう。

It was not. There were constant riots before the Japanese annexation during the Yi dynasty, casualties in the tens of thousands, hundreds of thousands were common.

しかしそうではありませんでした。朝鮮併合前、李氏朝鮮の時代には絶え間なく暴動があり、何万、何十万という死者が出るのが当たり前でした。

In a 1948 revolt across South Korea, President Rhee Syngmun killed 60,000 in Cheju Island alone.

1948年に韓国で全国的に起きた暴動で、李承晩大統領は済州島だけで6万人を殺害しました。

Japan subdued Korea's guerillas
朝鮮人ゲリラを抑えた日本

During the Korean War, guerrillas fought in the south until 1956. They were both local guerrillas and remnants of the North Korean People's Army that had driven south in 1950.

朝鮮戦争の間、1956年までゲリラが韓国内で戦闘していました。戦闘していたのは、韓国内のゲリラと1950年に韓国に攻め込んだ北朝鮮軍の残党です。

Yet there were no active guerrillas at all in Korea throughout the annexation period. There were two resistance forces that I know of. There was a guerrilla group in Manchuria. They never numbered more than 1,500. In a memoir by one of their members, "A North Korean remembers", he described one of their forays into Korea proper. He said that they did not dare approach a farmhouse for food or help even in the most remote areas.

それでも併合時代を通して、朝鮮で活動しているゲリラは全くいませんでした。私の知っている限りでは、二つのゲリラグループがありました。満洲に一つのグループがあり、最も人数が多い時で1,500人程度でした。そのグループの一人の手記「北朝鮮人は記憶している」で、彼は当時韓国に侵入した話を書いています。最も辺鄙な地域の農家にでさえ、朝鮮人ゲリラは食料や援助を求めて近づく勇気さえなかったと言っています。

The reason was that the farmer would inform the governmental police. Now critics of Japan here will say that this was because the Japanese police were too brutal, and the people were afraid.

　その理由は、農家は警察に通報しただろうからです。ここで、日本に批判的な解説者は、日本の警察が残虐で、民衆は怖かったからだと言います。

No. Since guerrilla war is people's war, it does not work like that. You cannot destroy the will of people to fight by force.

　違います。ゲリラ戦は人民の戦争ですから、そんなことはありません。人民の戦う意志を、力ずくで奪うことはできません。

Let us take a quick look at the US effort in the Vietnam War. The United States had some 9 Army divisions plus one Marine division in Vietnam. There were also some 13 South Vietnamese divisions plus other troops. Yet they could never eliminate resistance in Southern Vietnam. Eventually the Americans withdrew, abandoning the South Vietnamese government.

　ベトナム戦争でのアメリカの努力を見てみましょう。アメリカはベトナムに陸軍9個師団、海兵隊1個師団を投入し、南ベトナム軍は13個師団その他が配備されていました。しかし、これだけの大軍でも、南ベトナムでの抵抗を排除することは不可能でした。結局、数年後にアメリカは撤退し、南ベトナム政府は見捨てられました。

A US division is about 20,000 men.

　アメリカの1個師団は約2万人です。

The number of Japanese Imperial Army troops in Korea during the annexation period was at most one or two divisions. A Japanese division at the time was about 10,000 men. If Korea had been in constant revolt, a force of something like 10 to 15 divisions would have been required to keep order. As we have seen in Mr. Ireland's book, there was a slight majority of Japanese to Korean police in Korea in 1922. But as time went on, the number of ethnic Koreans increased in the police.

　併合時代の朝鮮半島にいた日本陸軍は最大でも１～２個師団だけでした。当時、日本の師団は１万人ほどでした。もし当時の朝鮮半島で頻繁に暴動が起きていたら、秩序を維持するのに10個から15個師団が必要だったでしょう。アイルランド氏の本を読むと、1922年の朝鮮の警察は、朝鮮人より日本人の数の方がやや多かったです。しかし時間と共に、朝鮮人の警官の数が多くなりました。

If there had been people's war in Korea, a revolt against Japanese rule, most of these ethnic Korean police would have taken their weapons and run to the mountains.

　もし当時、朝鮮において人民戦争、日本統治に対する反乱が起こっていたならば、この朝鮮人の警官のほとんどは武器を取り山へ逃げたでしょう。

If we look at a map, we can see that Korea is rather larger geographically than South Vietnam. Korea also has terrain ideally suited for guerrilla warfare. It has many rugged mountains.

　地図を見れば、当時の朝鮮の方が南ベトナムよりやや広いことが分かります。朝鮮半島の地勢を見ると、岩山が多く、ゲリラ戦にとても適しています。

If the Korean people had not acquiesced in Japanese rule, they would have taken to the mountains and fought. They had, many times in the past even with inferior weapons, fought with Yi dynasty government troops.

もし朝鮮の人々が日本統治に不満があったら、山にこもって戦ったでしょう。昔の朝鮮人は、劣った武器で過去幾度となく、李氏朝鮮の軍と戦っていました。

This did not happen. This was because the overwhelming majority of Korean people saw Japanese rule as a chance for a better life.

しかし、そんなことは起こりませんでした。圧倒的多数の朝鮮人は、日本統治の方がより良い生活ができる機会だと理解していたからです。

America could not provide that in Vietnam, so their effort failed.

アメリカはベトナムで日本のようなことができず、アメリカの努力は失敗に終わりました。

There was also another Korean Resistance Army based in Shanghai, but they never numbered more than 100 men or so.

上海にもう一つ朝鮮人の抗日組織がありましたが、その数はせいぜい100人程度を超えたことがありませんでした。

Yet, I have read articles where President Park Guen-Hye demands that Japan apologize for the resistance fighters killed fighting Japan.

にもかかわらず、韓国の朴槿恵大統領が、日本と戦って戦死した抗日兵士への謝罪を、日本に要求しているというマスコミの記事を読んだことがあります。

But there were not any such soldiers. Sorry to Korean people, but that is the truth. There was never any guerrilla fighting inside Korea whatsoever against the annexation to Japan. The Japanese annexation was the most peaceful and prosperous time in Korean history.

しかし、そんな兵士は存在していませんでした。韓国人にとっては残念ですが、それが真実です。朝鮮半島で日本への併合に抗するゲリラ戦は全くありませんでした。日本の併合時代は朝鮮の歴史の中で最も平和で、豊かな時代だったのです。

In 1910, when Japan annexed Korea, the population was 13,128,780 people. In 1942, it was 25,525,409 people. Under Japanese rule, the population doubled. If the Japanese military had been constantly raiding Korean villages for women, and there had been constant imprisonment and torture of Korean people as some people claim, the doubling of the population could not have happened.

1910年の併合時、朝鮮の人口は13,128,780人でしたが、1942年には25,525,409人に増えています。日本の統治で、人口が倍になったのです。もし日本軍が女を求めていつでも村を襲撃したり、ある人たちが主張するように、絶えず朝鮮人を刑務所で拷問にかけたりしていたなら、当時の朝鮮の人口は絶対に倍にはならなかったでしょう。

The Korean victimhood syndrome
韓国人の被害者意識

Why do Koreans hate Japan so much? I lived in Korea in the late 1970s. I remember a conversation I had with Korean friends one day. They asked me which country had the most difficult time in WWII.

どうして韓国人はそれほどまでに日本を憎んでいるのでしょうか？　私は1970年代後半に、韓国に住んでいました。ある日の、韓国人の友人たちとの会話を覚えています。彼らは、「第二次世界大戦でどこの国が最もつらい経験をしたと思うか？」と私に尋ねました。

Well, I thought that it was a very unusual question, in the year 1978. I answered Poland. Poland was invaded by both Germany and Russia. The German occupation lasted some 6 years, and yes, it was harsh. There were two great revolts in Poland, the Jewish Warsaw Uprising of 1943, and the Polish Guerrilla Home Army Warsaw Revolt of 1944.

1978年のことでしたが、どうしてそんなことを聞くのかなと思いました。私はポーランドだと答えました。ポーランドはドイツとロシアの両方から侵略されました。ドイツの占領は約6年間でしたが、それは本当に過酷なものでした。そのドイツ占領期間に二度、大きな武装蜂起が発生しています。1943年のワルシャワ・ゲットー蜂起と1944年の抵抗組織ポーランド国内軍によるワルシャワ蜂起がありました。

Both were crushed totally. And as the Russian Army advanced westward, the German Army fought tenaciously. All in all, 25% of Polish people died in the war.

どちらの蜂起も徹底的に鎮圧されました。その後、ロシア軍が徐々に西へと進撃し、ドイツ軍はポーランドに留まって頑強に戦いました。その結果、25%ものポーランド人の命が奪われました。

But when I said this, my Korean friends got very angry, and threatened me with violence. They screamed that Korea had the most difficult time in WWII. They were no longer my friends. And, these Korean people insulted the people of Poland.

しかし、私がこの話をすると、その韓国人の友人たちは激怒して、私に殴りかからんばかりの勢いで威圧してきました。第二次世界大戦では、韓国が一番大変だったんだと叫びました。彼らとはもう友達の縁を切りました。この韓国人たちはポーランド人に対してとても失礼です。

But this illustrates part of the inferiority/superiority complex that Koreans have.

しかしこれで、韓国人が持つ、劣等感・優越感の一端がよく分かります。

Korean superiority complex
韓国人の優越感

They have a huge superiority complex. They insist that Korea is the center of the world, that Seoul is the best place in the universe. Everything in the world began in Korea.

彼らはとてつもない優越感を持っています。韓国が世界の中心、ソウルが大宇宙の中で一番素晴らしい所だと力説します。世界の文明も発明も何もかも韓国が起源だと言います。

When I lived in Korea, Koreans would often demand to me that America adopt the Hangul writing system, because it is the best in the world. Well, for them it is OK, but I grew up with the Roman alphabet in America. It works well for America. I now live in Japan, and read and write using Chinese characters and the Japanese phonetic alphabets (i.e., hiragana, katakana).

私が韓国に住んでいた時に、韓国人が、よく私にアメリカはハングルを採用せよと要求してきました。世界でハングルが最も素晴らしい文字だからだそうです。まあ、韓国人にはハングルが良いと思いますが、私はアメリカでローマ字アルファベットで育ちました。アメリカでは、ローマ字アルファベットが良いでしょう。私は今日本に住んでいますので、書く時は、漢字、および日本の音標文字のひらがな、カタカナを使っています。

Another example is pizza. I watched this develop. In Korea, there is a dish called chijimi. It is made by frying vegetables, seafood or meat in batter, and looks like a flat pancake like dish.

もう一つ､ピザの話があります。私はこの話のなり行きを知っています。韓国にはチヂミという料理があります。小麦粉に卵を混ぜた生地に野菜、シーフード、肉を加えて焼いたもので、見た目は皿のように平らなパンケーキのような料理です。

When I lived in Korea, it was described to foreigners as Korean pizza. Over the years, this story has morphed into, "Marco Polo stole the concept of chijimi from Korea in his visit to Yi dynasty Korea!"

私が韓国に住んでいた時に、この料理は「コリアンピザ」だと外国人に説明しました。しかし何年か経つうちに、この話は､「マルコ・ポーロが李氏朝鮮に来た時に朝鮮からチヂミのアイデアを盗んだ！」になってしまいました。

Well, Marco Polo never visited Korea. But here we see this concept in the Korean mind that they are the victim. If somebody does some terrible wrong to them, they will think themselves as victims forever.

ところで、マルコ・ポーロは李氏朝鮮を訪問したことはありませんでした。でもこの話で、韓国人の「自分たちは犠牲者！」という意識がはっきり分かります。もし誰かが韓国人にひどいことをした場合、韓国人は永遠に自分が被害者だと考えます。

There are Koreans who also claim to have founded the Egyptian and Sumerian civilizations. They claim this because ancient texts say that Korea used to extend 40,000 ri (one ri is about 4 kilometers) from east to west.

エジプト文明とシュメール文明は、昔朝鮮人が創設したと主張している韓国人がいます。古文書に、昔の朝鮮は東西4万里に及んでいたと書かれているからだそうです（1里は約4キロです）。

Well, when the ancients wrote things, they wrote to make the king look great. They exaggerated. Modern-day historians understand this.

なるほど、古代の人が物を書く時、王が偉大に見えるように書きました。彼らが王の偉大さを誇張して書くことがあったことを、現代の歴史家は理解しています。

Koreans also claim the rights to Christmas trees around the world. The Korean National Institute of Biological Resources has said that DNA studies prove that the trees used for Christmas trees around the world originated in Korea. And that they should be paid copyright fees whenever they are used.

世界中で飾られているクリスマスツリーの権利を主張している韓国人もいます。韓国の生物資源研究所による遺伝子の分析で、世界のクリスマスツリーの木々の起源は韓国であることが証明されたということです。なので、木々を使う時には、韓国政府に著作権料を支払うべきであると言っています。

Therefore, every year when the President of the United States lights up the National Christmas Tree in front of the White House, will Korea send a bill?

それで、毎年、ホワイトハウスの前で、アメリカの大統領がナショナル・クリスマスツリーに点灯する度に、韓国政府は請求書を送ってくるのでしょうか？

Making wild baseless historical claims, and then demanding money is another unfortunate Korean trait. This is characteristic of the Japanese-Korean relationship.

でたらめな根拠のない歴史的主張をして、お金を要求する。これがもう一つの韓国人の残念な特性です。そういうことが日韓関係を特徴づけるものです。

Examining the "Comfort Women" issue
慰安婦問題を検証する

Let us look at some of the things that Koreans say happened during Japanese rule. First of all, the Comfort Women issue.

それでは、韓国人が日本統治時代に起こったこと主張していることを見ていきましょう。まず、慰安婦問題です。

Koreans say that some 200,000 women were dragged from their villages through the land, from the arms of wailing relatives, by Japanese Imperial Army troops. They were then taken to military brothels, where they were forced to have sex with as many as 40 men a day.

韓国人が言うには、大日本帝国陸軍の部隊が朝鮮全域の村々で、泣き叫ぶ家族の元から約 200,000 人の女性を無理やり拉致しました。そして、その女性たちは軍専用の売春宿へ強制連行され、1 日に 40 人もの男たちとのセックスを強要

郵便はがき

料金受取人払郵便

豊島局承認

3147

差出有効期間
2025年2月28日
まで

1708780

143

東京都豊島区池袋3-9-23

ハート出版

① 書籍注文 係
② ご意見・メッセージ 係（裏面お使い下さい）

〒

ご住所		
お名前		女・男 歳
電　話	－　－	
注文書	ご注文には電話番号が**必須**となりますので、ご記入願います。 お届けは**佐川急便**の「**代金引換**」となります。**代引送料￥600円＋税（代引手数料込）。** **離島**は日本郵便で、別途**追加料金**がかかる場合がございます。	
		冊
		冊
		冊

ご愛読ありがとうございます（アンケートにご協力お願い致します）

●ご購入いただいた書籍名は？

●本書を何で知りましたか？

① 書店で見て　② 新聞広告（紙名　　　　　　　　）

③ SNS等　④ その他（　　　　　　　　）

●購入された理由は？

①著者　②タイトルや装幀　③興味あるジャンル・内容　④人から薦められて

⑤ネットでの紹介・評価　⑥その他（　　　　　　　　）

●購入された書店名は？

区

市

町

ご意見・著者へのメッセージなどございましたらお願い致します

ありがとうございました

※お客様の個人情報は、個人情報に関する法令を遵守し、適正にお取り扱い致します。
ご注文いただいた商品の発送、その他お客様へ弊社及び発送代行からの商品・サービスのご案内をお送りすることのみに使用させていただきます。第三者に開示・提供することはありません。

されました。

If girls disobeyed, they were rolled naked across beds of nails, and boiled to death. The other girls were forced to eat of the human flesh of them by Japanese soldiers.

もしその女性が命令に従わない場合、釘のベッドの上を裸のまま転がされ、そして死ぬまでゆでられました。他の女性たちは、日本兵にその肉を食べるよう強要されました。

This is total fantasy. The Japanese Imperial Army never ever went into Korean villages. Internal order in Korea was basically kept by police. As we have seen, in 1922, in statistics provided by Alleyne Ireland in his work "The New Korea", nearly half of the police in Korea were ethnic Koreans.

これは完全なファンタジーです。大日本帝国陸軍の部隊は村に侵入していません。朝鮮国内の秩序は基本的に警察が守っていました。アレン・アイルランド氏の本「The New Korea」の統計によると、1922年の時点で警察官の約半数は朝鮮人でした。

As time went on, this percentage increased until the majority of police under Japanese rule were ethnic Koreans. If the police, who were in fact Koreans, actually did enter villages and drag off young women, the people did not resist?

時間が経つにつれ、朝鮮人の警察官の数が増えて、大多数の警察官は朝鮮人になりました。警察官が（その多くは朝鮮人ですが）、村に侵入して女性を強制連行しても、村の人々は抵抗しないのでしょうか？

There was only one significant nationwide riot under Japanese rule, the March 1919 incident. Under Yi dynasty rule, and in postwar Korea, violent protests were common. Then, why didn't the Korean people violently resist the Japanese government?

日本統治時代では、重要な全国的騒擾は一つだけで、1919年３月の事件しかありませんでした。李氏朝鮮時代、そして大東亜戦争後、韓国では暴力的な抗議運動はよく発生していました。それでは、どうして朝鮮人は日本政府には抵抗しなかったのでしょうか。

Some Western fans of Korea might say that Japanese were horribly violent people. But if Koreans were terrified of Japan and were timid pussy cats, yet were they ferocious tigers before and after Japanese rule? This does not make sense. I know Korean people, believe me, they would fight if such a horrible thing, the kidnapping of women, happened in their village.

韓国を支持する西洋人は、「日本人が恐ろしく暴力的な国民だから」と言うかもしれません。しかし、日本統治の時代は、朝鮮人は臆病な猫ちゃんなのに、その前後の期間は、獰猛な虎だったのでしょうか？　それでは筋が通りません。私は韓国人を理解しています。本当に、もし自分の村で女性が拉致されたら、彼らは戦いますよ！

Many foreigners, particularly American feminist activists, focus on the issue of coercion in the Comfort Women issue. They condemn prostitution, and apply standards of today to the issue.

多くの外国人、特にアメリカのフェミニスト活動家は、慰安婦問題では、強制性を中心に問題視しています。売春業を非難して、現在の価値基準をそのまま昔に適用しています。

Well, it was a fact that in both Japan and Korea at that time, a father could and often did sell a pretty daughter into prostitution due to poverty. In Japan, this practice no longer exists, and is forbidden by law. There is a thriving sex industry in Japan, but it is totally voluntary for women to enter the industry, and illegal acts are monitored by the police.

まあ、当時日本でも朝鮮でも、貧困が原因で、父親は家族のために娘を売り売春させることができたし、しばしばそうしたことは事実でした。現在の日本ではもうありませんし、法律で禁止されています。日本には大きなセックス産業がありますが、女性がその業界に入るのは自分の意志であり、違法行為は警察が取り締まっています。

US troops and Korean prostitutes
米兵と韓国人売春婦

I visited a Comfort Women station in Korea in 1977. It was outside the American Air Force base of Kunsan, in southwest Korea. The name of the area was Silvertown. It was in the middle of rice fields, surrounded by high walls, with a guarded gate.

私は1977年に韓国の慰安所へ行ったことがあります。韓国南西の群山米空軍基地の外にありました。その慰安所は「Silvertown」と呼ばれていました。周りは田んぼで、周囲を高い壁で囲まれていて、門は警備されていました。

The gate was guarded by a Korean government security guard, and a uniformed, armed US Air Force military police man. US Air Force medical officers checked the girls for sexual diseases. But this made sense. Before the establishment of Silvertown, US military personnel would hunt for sex in drinking places in the town. This led to much fighting and trouble with the local Korean people.

門に韓国政府の警備員１人と、制服を着て武装した米空軍の憲兵１人がいました。米空軍の軍医たちが、そこにいる女性の性病検査を行いました。しかし、この慰安所ができたことには意味がありました。「Silvertown」が設立される前は、米兵は街の飲み屋でセックスの相手をあさっていました。それが原因で、地元の韓国人とよく喧嘩になり、トラブルが数多く発生しました。

Some girls were indeed prostitutes, but most in the city of Kunsan were not. Drunken US military personnel did not differentiate. Therefore, to avoid trouble, Silvertown was established in an isolated area outside the city.

群山市には本当の売春婦もいましたが、ほとんどの女性はそうではありません。酔った米兵はそれを区別しませんでした。それで、トラブルを避けるために、街の郊外の孤立した場所に「Silvertown」が造られたのです。

And girls were still sold in Korea in the 1970's. If an American military man wanted to marry a Korean bar girl, he had to pay off her debt to the bar before the girl could leave the country. This is because the girls had been sold by their families.

1970年代、韓国では女性の人身売買がまだありました。米兵が韓国人のバーホステスと結婚したい場合、その女性が出国する前に、彼女の借金を、彼女が働くバーの主人に支払う必要がありました。女性たちは家族に売られてきたからです。

Of course, most Korean girls who married American military men were not prostitutes. But in America, all such Korean women who married American military men suffer extreme prejudice in the Korean communities in America.

もちろん、米兵と結婚した大抵の韓国女性は売春婦ではありませんでした。しかし、アメリカでは米兵と結婚した韓国人女性全員が、アメリカの韓国人社会でひどい差別を受けています。

I can attest to the veracity of US military causing trouble with women. When I was based in Japan, I traveled much throughout Japan as a US Marine. At first, I would invite other Marines to go with me, but they would always grab some girl by force, drag her to me and, since I spoke Japanese, ask me to explain to her that she should have sex with him.

私は米兵がなぜ女性と問題を起こすのか、その真相を証言できます。私は米海兵隊員として来日した時に、日本のあちこちを旅しました。最初の頃は、他の海兵隊員を一緒に行こうと誘いました。するといつも、どこへ行っても、女性の手首を掴んで私の所まで引っ張ってきて、日本語ができる私に、自分とセックスするよう伝えてほしいと言ってきました。

I would pass over my English-Japanese dictionary and tell him to do it himself. After a few bad experiences like that, I traveled alone in Japan.

私は自分の英和辞書を渡して、「自分で言え」と言いました。何度かそんな嫌な経験をしたので、一人で日本を旅しました。

American Feminists will not like this, but this is reality. This kind of thing has happened outside military camps since the dawn of humanity.

アメリカのフェミニストはこういうことは嫌いだと思います。でも、それが現実です。人類の夜明けから、軍のキャンプの周りでは、こういうことが起きているのです。

And such things still continue today. Girls who get into debt in Korea, for example with credit cards, are told that there is one way to pay it off, become a prostitute overseas, in Japan, America, Australia or Europe.

現在でも同じような事が続いています。韓国で、クレジットカードなどで借金を抱えてしまい、完済の方法が一つだけあると言われた女性は、日本、アメリカ、オーストラリアあるいはヨーロッパといった海外で売春婦になります。

Today in the US, 24% of trafficked foreign women come from South Korea.

現在のアメリカにおける、人身売買された外国人女性の24%は、韓国から来ています。

The truth of the "Comfort Women" issue
慰安婦問題の真実

But in Korea during the annexation to Japan, there were no forcible roundups of Korean women to be prostitutes. In fact, there were open advertisements in newspapers, detailing the salary to be expected. The pay for Comfort Women was extremely good, much better than the pay for Japanese enlisted troops.

しかし、日本の併合時代、朝鮮の女性を強制連行して売春婦にするということはありませんでした。実は、新聞に広告が出され、給料がはっきり書かれていました。慰安婦の給料はとても良く、日本軍兵士よりはるかに高給でした。

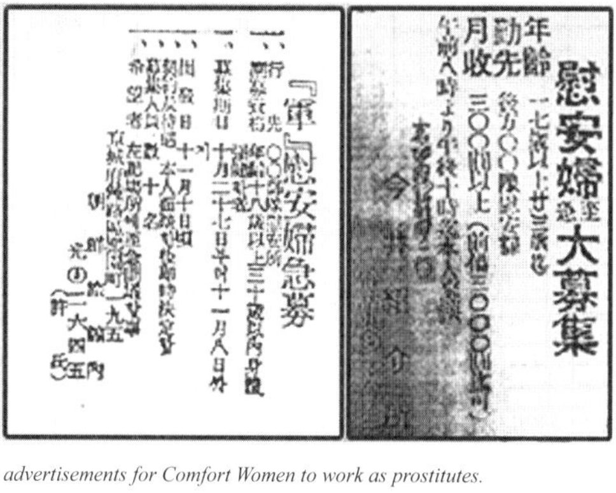

Newspaper advertisements for Comfort Women to work as prostitutes.

慰安婦募集の公告。朝鮮総督府機関誌「毎日新報」（左）と新聞「京城日報」。後者には月収 300 円以上（前借 3000 円まで可）と書かれている。

There were ethnic Koreans who used deceptive methods to recruit prostitutes, but they were arrested and prosecuted by the Japanese government.

　詐欺的な方法で売春婦を集める朝鮮人がいましたが、日本政府によって逮捕、起訴されました。

Comfort Women had home leave, and could socialize with Japanese soldiers in their free time. In fact, they had more privileges than American Comfort Women.

　慰安婦は休暇で故郷に帰ったり、休みの日に日本兵と普通に付き合ったりすることもできました。実際、アメリカの慰安婦より多くの特権がありました。

Yes, American did have an organized system of government sponsored prostitution. It was in Hawaii during the Pacific War. The Hawaiian territorial government knew that when the war started, many drunken service men on their way to war would pass through Hawaii. They did not want these troops in the better parts of Honolulu, where their wives and daughters lived.

　そうです。アメリカには政府出資の組織化された売春システムがあり、大東亜戦争の時にハワイで運営されていました。ハワイ準州政府は、戦争が始まれば、飲んだくれのアメリカ兵が大勢ハワイ経由で前線へ行くということを知っていたので、彼らの妻や娘が住むホノルルの優良な地域に、そんな米兵が来て欲しくありませんでした。

As a result, down near the port, “Hotel Street” was created. The

US military, Hawaiian Territorial government, and Hawaiian police all cooperated in this effort. The hotels were already there. Being American, things were on an assembly line basis. The military man would go into the room, strip, and wash his private parts with disinfectant. The girl would come in, put a condom on the service man, and then he had 3 minutes.

それで、港の近くに「ホテルストリート」が作られました。これには米軍、ハワイ準州政府、ハワイ警察が協力しました。そのホテル街は以前からありました。アメリカ式なので、ことは工場の流れ作業のように行われていました。兵士は部屋に入り、服を脱いで、消毒液で自分の下半身を洗います。女性が部屋に入ってきて、兵士にコンドームを付け、それから3分でセックスを済ませます。

US sailors lining up outside the" Hotel Street" or an American Comfort women establishment in Honolulu, Hawaii.

ハワイ、ホノルルの慰安施設、「ホテルストリート」の外で行列する米海軍の水兵たち。

The military called these troops “3 minutes’ men”. They referred to Hotel Street as the area to get lubed, screwed, and tattooed. To lube means to lubricate or get intoxicated with alcoholic drink, to screw means to have sex with someone, and to tattoo means to create a permanent picture or word on the surface of skin by using needles to put colors under the skin. The American women would do 100 men a day.

こういう兵士のことを軍隊の俗語で「3分の男」と呼びました。ホテルストリートは「lubed, screwed, and tattooed」する所だと言われました。lube は潤滑油をさす、つまりお酒を飲む、screw はセックスする、tattoo は刺青を入れる、という意味です。このアメリカの売春婦は1日に100人もの相手をしました。

They made a lot of money, but the labor conditions were strict. They could not own a house or car, and could not leave the area of Hotel Street. Most of these women were professional prostitutes from San Francisco.

売春婦たちはかなりのお金を儲けましたが、労働条件は厳しいものでした。車も家も所有することを禁止され、ホテルストリートの区域から出ることも禁止されていました。この女性たちは大部分がサンフランシスコから来たプロの売春婦でした。

Many Japanese and ethnic Comfort Women did have contracts that they were obligated to serve out. Their families had received money from brokers, so it had to be paid back.

日本人および少数民族の慰安婦は、契約した期間、奉仕する義務がありました。慰安婦の家族は、ブローカーからお金を貰っていたので、それを返済しなければなりませんでした。

But the Japanese system was safe and clean. There was none of the brutality that Koreans say happened.

しかし、日本のシステムは安全で衛生的でした。韓国人が言うような虐待はありませんでした。

And today, the Korean former Comfort Women give very emotional heart-wrenching performances. Yet I have read of people having witnessed the women, after the performance, coming around to the back entrance of the venue where the event was held, and being given envelopes of money.

現在、元韓国人慰安婦はとても感情的で胸が痛むパフォーマンスを行っています。しかし、私が読んだ記事では、パフォーマンスが終わると、その元慰安婦たちはイベント会場の裏口で、お金が入った封筒をもらっているのを目撃した人々のことが書かれていました。

And I have seen photos of the same women, sometimes she is in a wheelchair, and who also sometimes walks just fine. This is a staged show, an act, designed to get the sympathy of Westerners who do not have much knowledge about recent Asian history.

私も、ある時は車椅子、ある時は元気に歩いている、同じ女性の写真を見たことがあります。これは芝居で、東洋の近現代史を知らない西洋人の同情を買うために演じています。

Did Japan destroy Korea's culture?
日本は本当に朝鮮の文化を破壊したのか？

Koreans also claim that Japan destroyed their culture. Well, Japan revived the Korean alphabet, while the Yi dynasty Yangban had let it go out of use. The only education in Yi dynasty Korea was in Chinese characters.

韓国人は日本が自分たちの文化を破壊したと主張しています。李氏朝鮮の両班がハングルを相手にせず、だんだん使われなくなりましたが、日本が統治時代にハングルを復興させました。李氏朝鮮の時代の教育は漢字のみでした。

When the French colonized Vietnam, they discouraged or banned the use of Chu Nom, the Chinese ideograph based Vietnamese writing.

フランス人がベトナムを植民地にした時は、漢字をベースにしたチュノムというベトナム文字の使用を妨げたり禁止したりしました。

Vietnamese then embraced Roman letters. Today few can read the old Chu Nom texts. But unlike Koreans who always complain about Japan, Vietnamese do not roam the world crying about the French.

ベトナム人は、ローマ字を受け入れました。現在、チュノム文献を読めるベトナム人はごくわずかです。でも、いつも日本に文句を言う韓国人とは異なり、ベトナム人は世界中でフランス人の悪口を触れ回ったりしません。

If Japan had truly banned Hangul, almost nobody could have read it in 1945 after 35 years of annexation, when Japan surrendered and Korea was transferred to the control of the United States and Soviet Russia. Yet at that time most Koreans were literate in Hangul and Japanese both.

　もし日本が本当にハングルを禁止していたら、併合から35年後、日本が降伏して米ソが朝鮮を支配するようになった時に、ほとんどの朝鮮人がハングルを読めなかったでしょう。しかし、1945年当時の大抵の朝鮮人は日本語とハングルの両方を読めました。

It is Japan's introducing a mass education system that was revolutionary in creating a Korea where all Koreans could prosper regardless of class, at least in postwar South Korea.

　日本は統治した朝鮮に、革新的な大衆教育システムを導入しました。これにより、全ての朝鮮人は階級に関係なく誰でも豊かな生活ができる可能性が生まれました、少なくとも戦後の韓国では。

I do know of one practice that Japan did ban during this period, which has been revived as a Korean folk dance today. This is the Byeongsin chum, or dance to mock the handicapped. I have problems with this. I have seen YouTube videos of this dance, and I cannot find anything to admire here. The Wikipedia entry says that its purpose is to satirize the nobility. But the more you study Korea, the more you find a cruel streak in Korea society.

　私は、李氏朝鮮のある習慣が併合後に禁止されたことを知っています。現在、韓国で民族舞踊として復活しています。

それは、病身舞という踊りで、体の不自由な人を嘲るものです。私はこの踊りが嫌いです。YouTubeで見ましたが、どこがいいのか分かりません。ウィキペディアでは、この踊りの本当の意味は貴族たちに対する風刺である、と書いています。しかし、コリアをより深く研究すると、コリア社会の残酷な面が益々いろいろと見えてきます。

Japan was correct to ban this practice.

日本がこの踊りを禁止したのは、正しいことでした。

Koreans also say that they were forced to speak Japanese. Well, since Korea was very hierarchal under the Yi Dynasty, it was natural that Japanese speaking Koreans would consider themselves superior to those who could not. This is part of the fabricated story of destroying Korean culture.

韓国人の話では、日本人から、日本語を使うよう強制されたと言います。まあ李氏朝鮮は非常に階級的な社会でしたから、併合時代の朝鮮で日本語ができる朝鮮人は、できない朝鮮人に対して優越感を持てたでしょう。これは、日本が朝鮮の文化を潰したという、嘘だらけの話の原因の一つです。

In the same way in Japan, in the post-Pacific War American occupation and American dominance era. Japanese people who could speak English had much status in Japan. But that time is ending, and Japanese people are losing interest in America and speaking English.

日本も同じです。大東亜戦争後、アメリカの占拠時代とアメリカの日本支配時代、日本では英語を喋る人が幅を利かせていました。しかし、その時代も終わり、だんだん日本人はアメリカや、英語を喋ることに興味を失っています。

In any case, Koreans certainly did not forget to speak Korean, so it must have been used on daily basis during the annexation. And the truth is most Japanese people who moved to Korea during that period, learned to speak Korean.

いずれにしても、当時の朝鮮人は当然朝鮮語を話すことを忘れなかったので、併合時代、毎日使っていたに違いありません。そして、併合時代に朝鮮に渡った大部分の日本人が、朝鮮語を学んで話せたという事実があります。

The truth about the adoption of Japanese names
創氏改名の真実

Another big complaint of the Koreans is that Japan forced people to adopt Japanese names. No. It was voluntary.

もう一つ、韓国人が強く訴えているのは、日本が朝鮮人に日本人の名前を使うように強制した、というものです。違います。自由意志によるものでした。

But Koreans still use Japanese names today. Yes, in America. I have seen advertisements for massage parlors, which are really centers of Korean prostitution. They always use names like Sakura, Tokyo, Nagoya, Osaka or something.

しかし、韓国人は現代でも日本の名前を使っています。アメリカでの話です。私は韓国系のマッサージパーラーの広告を見たことがあります。実際はそこで韓国人による売春が行われています。よく使われる店の名前は、さくら、東京、大阪、名古屋などです。

First of all, in Japanese, it comes off as tacky. But nowhere do I see a Korean massage parlor with a name like Seoul, Pusan, or Taegu. Why? Aren't the Korean people proud of their culture. Well, they have much pride, but also, a tremendous inferiority complex towards Japan.

まず、日本語でこのように店に地名を付けるのはお洒落とは言えませんが、それにしても韓国のソウル、釜山、大邱という名前を使っている韓国系のマッサージパーラーを私は見たことがありません。韓国人は自分の文化に強い誇りがないのでしょうか？　まあ、誇りはあるのですが、日本に対して、とても強い劣等感を持っているのです。

I have also seen Korean canned goods labeled with Japanese names like Geisha, or Sakura.

私は、芸者、さくらなどの日本の名称をつけた韓国の缶詰も見たことがあります。

The Koreans claim that they are the source of Japanese culture
韓国人による自分たちこそ日本文化の起源との主張

Koreans claim that many aspects of Japanese culture originated in Korea. They claim that Samurai came from the Saulabi, who were the original such warriors in the ancient Baekje kingdom. There is no evidence to support this.

韓国人はよく、日本の文化の様々な面は韓国が起源だと主張しています。彼らは、日本の武士、侍の起源は、百済の「サウラビ」であると主張します。しかし証拠はありません。

They claim to have originated the Japanese tea ceremony. I have seen a video of a Korean tea ceremony, where they use a metal thermos for the hot water. Since that would be an incredible rudeness in Japan, no Japanese would perform it in that way.

韓国人は日本の茶道の起源も韓国だと言います。その韓国茶道のビデオを見たことがありますが、お湯は魔法瓶に入っていました。日本では、それは途方もなく失礼なことなので、日本人は絶対にそのようなことをしません。

And of course, they claim that cherry trees, popular for viewing their spring flowers bloom in Japan, originated from Korea.

それに日本のソメイヨシノ、春のお花見でも大人気ですが、彼らは、朝鮮半島が起源だと言います。

These cultural claims do make the Korean people unique, which is not a good way. It is a sign of mental illness on a national scale. No other countries with a rivalry with another nation do such things.

このような主張をするのは、世界で韓国人だけです。しかしこれは良い話ではありません。国家規模の精神疾患の兆候です。他国とライバル関係にあるどの国だって、こんなことはやりません。

For example, the English have a long-time great rivalry with the French. But any English person will freely admit that French cuisine is much superior to British. They will also say that the French language is more beautiful than English to the ear. Since I am a native speaker of English, and also a French speaker, I agree with this. And no English person would try to imitate and pass themselves off as French.

たとえば、英国人とフランス人は、昔から強力なライバル関係にあります。でも、英国人の誰でも、英国料理よりフランス料理の方が美味しいことを率直に認めますし、英語よりフランス語の方が綺麗に聞こえると言います。私は英語が母国語ですが、フランス語もできますので、この意見には同意します。しかし、英国人がフランス人を真似たり、なりすますようなことは絶対にしません。

Koreans in other countries all the time are prone to say that they are Japanese.

韓国人は、他国でよく自分は日本人だと言います。

Rampant persecutions in the name of patriotism
「愛国無罪」の手に負えない迫害

Of course, not all Koreans have such feelings of hatred for Japan. But to express that concept can be dangerous. In 2013, in a park in Seoul, a 95-year-old man was beaten to death by a man in his

30s. The reason was because the old man said that the Japanese annexation period benefited Korea. The young man said that he felt uncontrollable anger, and killed him.

もちろん、全ての韓国人が日本に対して嫌悪感を持っているわけではありません。しかし、韓国国内で、そんな感情をはっきり出すのは危険です。2013年にソウルの公園で、30代の男性が95歳の男性を殴り殺しました。その老人が併合は韓国にとって良いことだったと言ったからです。その30代の男性は、怒りを抑えられず、その老人を殺してしまったと言いました。

The judge said that the young man's actions were understandable, and gave him a 5 years' sentence, very light for murder.

裁判官はその男性の犯行に到った動機は理解できると言い、懲役5年を宣告しました。殺人事件としては、非常に軽い刑でした。

I thought that old people were respected in Korea, a country that treasures the teaching of Confucius.

私は、儒教の教えを大切にしている韓国の人々は、お年寄りを尊敬していると思っていました。

I have seen photos on the net, of a Seoul university professor being beaten and forced to bow in apology to former Comfort Women. The reason was because he said in his research that he could find no evidence of Japanese military or government coercion.

　ネットで、ソウル大学の教授が殴られ、元慰安婦の前で土下座を強要されている写真を見ました。その教授の調査では、日本政府・日本軍が慰安婦を強制連行した証拠は見つからなかった、と発言したのが原因でした。

I thought that teachers were respected in Korea, a country that treasures the teaching of Confucius.

　私は、儒教の教えを大切にしている韓国の人々は、学校の先生を尊敬していると思っていました。

I have frequently heard many such stories from Japanese who have Korean friends that Koreans fear for their lives in South Korea if they speak about Japan in a positive way.

　他にも、韓国で日本のことを肯定的に話したら殺されかねないと危険を感じるという話を、韓国人の友人がいる日本人からよく耳にします。

Korean actions have blowback
韓国人の自業自得

Anti-Japanese sentiment is reaching a level of hysteria in Korea today. Those Comfort Women statues spreading around the world, they are beginning to look like some sort of cult.

　今日、韓国の反日感情はヒステリーのレベルになっています。世界中に広がる慰安婦像は、まるでカルトのようです。

This has already had a very negative impact on Japanese-Korean relations. Up until a few years ago, there was a Korean cultural boom in Japan. Korean dramas were popular on TV. K-pop stars and Korean stars had masses of Japanese fans.

この問題が、日韓関係にとても悪い影響を及ぼしています。数年前まで、日本は韓流ブームでした。韓国のテレビドラマは日本で人気でしたし、K-POPスターや韓流映画スターが数多くの日本人ファンを獲得しました。

Many Japanese traveled to South Korea to tour the area where those dramas were filmed. Korean food and Korean language classes were popular in Japan.

多くの日本人が、そのドラマロケ地を見に韓国に観光旅行していましたし、韓国料理、韓国語のクラスも日本で人気でした。

That is all over. The Korean hysteria over the Comfort Women issue and their nasty treatment of Japanese people has backfired. Now, Japanese tourists shun Korea as a destination, and their tourist industry is in collapse.

それが急速に萎んでしまいました。韓国人の慰安婦問題におけるヒステリーと、日本人に対するひどい扱いが、この失敗に繋がりました。現在、日本人観光客は行先として韓国を避け、韓国の観光業界は崩壊しています。

And the Korea people express bewilderment at this. Are they really that stupid? Apparently, due to their groundless feelings of superiority, they felt that no matter how insulting they acted toward Japanese people, Japanese would still come to Korea for sightseeing and spend money.

韓国人はそのことに困惑を表します。しかし、どうしてそうなったのか、分からないのでしょうか？　やはり、自分たちの方が上位であるという根拠のない優越感があり、日本人にはどんな失礼な態度をとっても、日本人はまた韓国へ観光にきて、お金を落とすと思っていたのでしょう。

What do I mean?

何を言いたいのかと言えば、以下のような事件がありました。

In 2015, Mr. Kato Tatsuya, of the Sankei newspaper, was forbidden to leave Korea. He was accused of defamation. His crime was to reprint an article, written by a Korean reporter about the whereabouts of President Park for a few hours during the Sewol ferry disaster. The Korean reporter was never charged with any crime.

2015年に、産経新聞の加藤達也さんが韓国から出国禁止の命令を受けました。名誉毀損で告発されたのです。その理由は、韓国人記者が韓国語で書いた記事を、翻訳して記事にしたことです。内容は、セウォル号フェリー転覆事故の時の、数時間に亘る朴槿恵大統領の所在についてもので、元の記事を書いた韓国人記者は告発されませんでした。

But he was told by the Korean prosecution that if he admitted to wrong doing, and paid a fine, he could leave Korea and return to Japan. I thought that this kind of shakedown only would happen in corrupt kleptocratic third world countries.

　しかし、加藤さんは韓国の検察から、悪いことをしたと認めて、罰金を払えば、韓国を出て日本に帰ることができると言われました。私は、このようなゆすり行為は、第三世界の腐敗した略奪国家でしか起こらないと思っていました。

Eventually after some months Mr. Kato was found not guilty at first trial and the Korean prosecution abandoned the appeal.

　結局数ヵ月後、一審で無罪判決が出され、韓国の検察は控訴を断念しました。

But these bizzarre actions has made Korea unpopular as a tourist destination.

　しかし、こういう異常なことが次々起きたせいで、韓国はもう観光スポットとしての人気がなくなりました。

And now the Korean tourist industry is near collapse. Korea is descending into rule of the thug.

　こうなると、韓国の観光業はまもなく崩壊するでしょう。韓国は悪党が支配する社会になり下がっています。

The Korean poop fetish
韓国人の「大便フェチ」

In fact, Korean people seem to be de-evolving, regressing. They are becoming infantile. I think that it is now time to write about the poop fetish.

　実際に、韓国人は退化しているように見えますし、幼稚になっています。事ここに至ると、大便フェチについて書くべきと考えます。

Now it may surprise you that I bring up such a subject in a book like this. But truly, South Koreans are infatuated with feces. There is a cafe in central Seoul called Ddong cafe, with all kinds of goods throughout the establishment, like pooping dolls, toilet plungers, and works made in the motif of toilets.

　読者の皆さんは、このような本でそのような話題を持ち出すことに驚かれるかもしれません。しかし本当に、韓国人は大便が大好きなんです。ソウルの中心に、Ddong カフェという所があります。店のあちこちに、大便をしている人形、トイレ用吸引カップ、便器をモチーフにした作品など様々なグッズがあります。

They sell ddongbang, poop-shaped pastries. There is a popular character in Korean culture called Dongchimee, which we translate as “Poop man”. And the Poop Man doll is capable of performing the act of defecation. There is also a girl doll that does the same thing.

店では、ddongbangという大便の形をした菓子を売っています。Dongchimeeという韓国の人気キャラクターの商品もありますが、それは大便男という意味です。その大便男の人形は排便することができます。同様の女の子の人形もあります。

South of Seoul, in the city of Suwon there is a museum that is dedicated to toilet affairs that has many statues of people in the act of defecation. There are also smaller museums across the country.

ソウルの南の水原市にあるトイレ博物館には、排便中の人物の像がたくさんあります。規模はそれより小さいですが、韓国中に同じテーマの博物館があります。

And it is not only in museums that this poop fetish exists. Taekwondo is considered the national martial art of Korea. This year, some Taekwondo competitor was dissatisfied with a ruling for election of directors by the Taekwondo council, and scattered feces and urine in the Taekwondo office building hallway before the board of directors.

この大便フェチは博物館だけの話ではありません。テコンドーは韓国の国技です。今年、テコンドー国技院の理事選出に不満があったテコンドー選手が、理事会が開催される時に、国技院の廊下に糞尿をまき散らしました。

Now, I cannot imagine an athlete from any other country doing such a thing.

　他の国で、スポーツ選手がそんなことをするなど想像できません。

The Korean cult of bashing Japan
韓国人の日本バッシング熱

Now South Korea is a country where its people have made a religion of attacking Japan. Comfort Women statues appear everywhere. I have seen photos of people speaking in Korea in front of Comfort Women statues over 5 meters in size.

　韓国では日本バッシングは宗教になっています。慰安婦像はどこでも出現します。韓国で5メートル超の慰安婦像の前で人がスピーチしている写真を見たことがあります。

The Comfort Women issue has become some kind of weird religion.

　慰安婦問題は、怪しげな宗教になっています。

In Seoul, the old city hall built in the Japanese annexation era, was too small, and so a new one had to be built. Many anti-Japanese South Koreans wanted to destroy it as a symbol of Japan, but other Koreans wanted to preserve it for its historical significance.

　ソウルの市庁舎は、併合時代に建設されたもので小さかったので、新しい庁舎が必要でした。多くの反日的な韓国人は、その建物は日本のシンボルだから解体したいと思っていましたが、歴史的重要性のある建物なので、残すべきであると考える韓国人もいました。

They won, and a new town hall was built behind it. However, it was built in the shape of a giant wave about to swallow the old building.

残すべきと考える人たちの意見が通り、新庁舎は旧庁舎の裏に建設されることになりました。しかし、新庁舎は、巨大な波が今にも旧庁舎を飲み込むかのような形だったのです。

In March of 2011 Japan suffered a terrible earthquake. Korean people celebrated this, calling it the punishment of heaven.

2011年３月に、日本で恐ろしい地震が発生しました。韓国人はこの災害を祝い、そして、天罰だと言いました。

But Koreans are not only nasty towards Japan. I remember the 2002 World Cup. Not only was the cheating and bribery by Korea massive, but their manners were atrocious.

しかし、韓国人は日本だけに卑劣なわけではありません。2002年のワールドカップを覚えています。これは大がかりな不正行為と賄賂の問題だけでなく、一般の韓国人のマナーも最悪でした。

I remember seeing a banner about 20 meters long, with “Go to hell” written in Italian during the Korean match against Italy. I think that 5 obvious goals by the Italian team were disqualified by the presumably bribed judge.

韓国対イタリアの試合では、20メートルの横断幕に、イタリア語で「地獄へ行け！」と書かれていました。その試合の審判は賄賂をもらっていたのだと思いますが、５つぐらいの明らかなイタリアのゴールを無効にしました。

I also remember seeing on TV vendors outside the stadium before the match against Germany. They were selling photos of the German team members with black funerary ribbons on them, a tremendous insult.

ドイツとの試合の前に、スタジアムの外にある売店がテレビに映りました。ドイツチームのメンバーの写真を販売していましたが、その写真は遺影のように黒いリボンを付けて売っていました。これは呆れるほど失礼なことです。

In almost any sporting event involving a Japanese team in South Korea, there is in most cases cheating by the Korean side, involved. In a badminton match, the competing teams switch sides halfway through. Well in the stadium in Korea, blowers had been set so as to blow against the Japanese, no matter which side of the net they were on.

日本も参加するスポーツの競技会が韓国で行われる場合、たいてい韓国サイドから何らかの不正行為があります。バドミントンの試合では、途中でコートチェンジを行います。しかし、その韓国の体育館では、コートのどちら側でも、日本側に強い向かい風が吹く空調操作が行われました。

But cheating is not limited to sports. I saw a video on YouTube about an internationally famous sweets contest named the

World Pastry Team Championship (WPTC) held in Phoenix, Arizona, USA in 2010. Among the 5 finalists creating fantastic desserts were teams from South Korea and Japan.

　不正行為はスポーツの世界だけではありません。YouTubeで、2010年にアメリカ、アリゾナ州フェニックスで行われた国際的に有名なスイーツ大会 World Pastry Team Championship（WPTC）2010の映像を見ました。豪華で素晴らしいデザートを作る５組の決勝戦出場チームの中に、韓国と日本チームがいました。

The Korean team leader boasted on camera how he would not let Japan beat them. But their cheating was spotted. The Korean team shared a freezer with the Japanese team. The Koreans kept the freezer door open for long lengths of time, so that the Japanese desert partially melted.

　韓国のチームリーダーが、カメラの前で日本には勝たせないと自慢げに話をしていました。しかし、韓国側に不正行為が見られました。日本チーム、韓国チームは同じ冷蔵庫を使っていましたが、韓国チームは、わざと長い時間冷蔵庫のドアを開けていたため、日本チームが作ったデザートが一部溶けてしまったのです。

The South Korean team was penalized. But the Japanese team made a little chocolate cup, which poured molten warm chocolate over the ruined desert, and won the contest.

　韓国チームはペナルティーを受けました。しかし、それでも日本チームは、その崩れたデザートに、小さなカップから温かいチョコレートソースを注ぐ斬新なアイデアもあって、優勝しました。

But Korean people, do you really believe that it is quite OK to cheat at events like a badminton match and a dessert contest if the opponent is Japanese?

しかし、韓国の皆さん、デザート世界大会やバドミントンの試合のように、相手が日本人なら不正をしても良いのだと、本当に思っているのですか？

Korean Anti-Japanese education
韓国における反日教育

The Korean education system teaches hatred of Japan and a glorification of Korea's role in the Pacific War. Koreans are taught that they were one of the Allied powers, but the truth is that they enthusiastically fought for Japan as Japanese.

韓国の教育システムでは、日本に対する憎しみと、大東亜戦争でのコリアの役割を美化して教えています。学校では、コリアは連合国の一つであると教えられますが、実際は、併合時代の朝鮮人は、日本人として日本のために一生懸命勇敢に戦いました。

Well, they were Japanese citizens at the time, of which present-day Koreans are ashamed.

ところで、当時朝鮮人は日本国民でした。現在の韓国人はこの事実を恥じています。

Some time ago I saw a Japanese TV broadcast. They went into a Korean primary school. The lesson being taught was that the leader of North Korea, Kim Jong Il, was a good man working for reunification.

少し前のことですが、韓国の小学校を訪問する日本のテレビ番組を見ました。その日の授業は、金正日という北朝鮮のリーダーは、再統一のために努力している良い人だという内容でした。

The teachers openly said in the interview that this was necessary to prepare for reunification.

インタビューで、韓国の学校の先生が、この教育は再統一の準備のために必要であると話していました。

I have seen on YouTube videos of Korean primary school students making paintings. The teachers encourage them. The paintings show Japan on fire, or Japan sinking. They were all terrible. Children at that age do not think of such things naturally. They are being taught to hate Japan.

YouTubeで、韓国人の小学生が絵を描いている映像を見たことがあります。先生たちが生徒を励ましています。そこには、日本が燃えている、あるいは沈没している絵が描かれています。全部恐ろしい絵でした。その年齢の子供が自然にそのようなことを考えるわけがありません。学校が日本を憎むよう教育しているからです。

The fact is that this is nothing resembling any truth. Korean educators teach false information for ideological reasons, not to teach truth. It is also the case with the anti-Japan education.

実際のところ、これは真実とは似ても似つかないものです。韓国の教育者は真実を教えるのではなく、イデオロギーのために嘘を教えています。反日教育もそうです。

And this anti-Japan education has produced a lot of people who take action against Japan.

この反日教育は、日本に対して行動を起こす人をたくさん生み出しました。

Koreans are jealous of Japanese culture, and so they want to destroy it. I have seen videos on the net of Koreans defacing books in a public library.

韓国人は日本の文化を妬んでいて、それらを崩壊させたいようです。ネット上のビデオで、韓国人が図書館にある本を改竄しているものを見ました。

In December of 2015 a Korean man planted a bomb inside a restroom at Yasukuni shrine in Tokyo. The bomb only partially exploded. He was arrested when he came back for a second try. In court, he said his motive was to become a famous hero in South Korea.

2015年12月に、韓国人男性が靖国神社のトイレに爆弾を仕掛けました。爆弾は不完全爆発でしたが、その犯人が、再度爆弾を設置しようと日本に入国した時に逮捕されました。裁判で、彼は韓国で英雄になりたいという動機からであったと述べました。

Vandalism of public library books, and setting bombs are crimes. What kind of country is it where committing a crime makes you a hero?

図書館の本を書き換える行為、爆弾設置は全て犯罪です。犯罪者が英雄になるとは、一体どういう国なんですか？

But is not this jealousy the true reason for Korean hatred of Japan? Japanese culture is respected the world over. The tale of Genji is renowned. Kabuki and Noh are attractive. Kyoto is an exquisite city. I have also been to Kyongju in Korea, but it just does not compare to Kyoto. And many other cities in Japan are indeed beautiful.

しかし、この嫉妬心が、韓国人が日本を憎悪する本当の理由ではないでしょうか？　世界中で日本の文化が尊敬されています。源氏物語は有名ですし、歌舞伎、能楽は魅力があります。京都は非常に美しい街です。韓国の慶州市に行ったことがありますが、比較になりません。そして、その他の日本の街も綺麗な所が多いです。

Well, why is this? It is because of the nature of Yi dynasty Korea, a top-down society where only the very elite could read. That is why a deep Korean culture could never really develop. To the Korean mind, thinking with a background of Confucianism, Japan must be an inferior barbarian nation in all respects.

これはなぜでしょうか？文字を読むことができたのはエリートだけであった李氏朝鮮という階層社会の性格に因るものです。それで、朝鮮の文化が深まることはありませんでした。儒教が根付いた韓国人の考えでは、日本はあらゆる点で劣った野蛮人の国でなければなりません。

Yet the truth is that in every way, Japan outshines Korea. And the best, most prosperous period in Korean history was under Japanese rule. This infuriates the Koreans.

しかし実際は、あらゆる点で日本は韓国より優れています。そして、コリアの歴史の中で、一番平和で、豊かな時代は日本統治時代でした。この事実は、韓国人を激怒させます。

"Korean fatigue" among foreigners
外国人の「韓国疲れ」

If Koreans kept this anti-Japanese irrational hate merely to themselves, it might not be such an issue. But Korean people are traveling the world, peddling false stories that Japan was so terrible to them.

もし韓国人が、その反日感情を内輪だけで留めていれば、大した問題ではなかったのかもしれません。しかし韓国人は世界中を巡り日本がコリアにひどいことをした、という嘘をまき散らしています。

The Comfort Women statue has become the symbol of some sort of weird religion. In photos, I see people covering the statue in Seoul with scarves and caps in the winter time. That is a form of worship. It is a totally exaggerated story, and Koreans look rather ridiculous.

　慰安婦像はある種の異様な宗教のシンボルになっています。冬、ソウルの慰安婦像に、スカーフが巻かれ帽子がかぶせられているのを写真で見ました。これはある種の崇拝です。完全に誇張された物語であり、韓国人が滑稽に見えます。

And how is the reception Koreans get from foreigners? Well, at first, they got sympathy. After all, very few Westerners understand the truth of the Pacific War. But gradually, they get tired of constant Korean stories about how bad Japan is.

　それでは、外国人は韓国人の話をどのように受け止めているのでしょうか？　ええ、最初は、同情しました。結局のところ、大東亜戦争の真実を知っている西洋人は殆どいませんから。しかし、韓国人があまりに「日本はひどい！」という話を繰り返すものだから、だんだんウンザリしてきています。

The thing is that Koreans are not doing anything to help their country themselves, but they are asking foreigners to attack Japan for them. This entire anti-Japan international effort is to seek foreign help for Korea to dominate Japan.

　問題は、韓国人は自分の国のために、自分で努力して何とかしようとせず、外国人の力を借りて日本を攻撃していることです。この国際的な韓国の反日活動は、韓国が日本より優位に立つために、外国人を利用しようというものです。

There is a word appearing now in Western writings about Korea, which is called Korea fatigue. They are getting tired of constant complaints about Japan.

韓国について西洋人が書いた本にこういう言葉があります。「韓国疲れ」というものです。外国人は、執拗に繰り返される日本批判に疲れています。

Personal memories of Korea
韓国に対する私の思い出

Some people may wonder why I am so critical of Korea, but I have a right. I can say that I fought for their country.

なぜ私がこんなに韓国に対して批判的なのかと思う人がいるかもしれません。しかし、私にはその権利があります。私は韓国のために戦ったと言えるからです。

In 1974, I joined the United States Marine Corps. In December of that year, I was sent to a Marine base in Japan. Since I learned Japanese very quickly, and worked in a headquarters office, the United States Communist Party tried to recruit me to be a spy. They disguised themselves as journalists near the base, where they kept offices.

1974年、私は米海兵隊に入隊しました。その年の12月、日本にある海兵隊の基地に派遣されました。私はすぐ日本語を覚えて、司令部の事務所で働いていましたが、アメリカ共産党は私にスパイになるように働きかけてきました。基地の近くに事務所があり、彼らはジャーナリストを装っていました。

The next day I reported this to my Marine Corps superiors, and became an undercover Naval Intelligence operative. What the Communists were doing was general espionage, helping US troops desert from Japan through Russia to Sweden to escape the Vietnam war, and looking for proof of nuclear weapons on US bases in Japan.

　次の日、私は上官にその経緯を報告し、米海軍情報部局の秘密捜査員になりました。日本にいたアメリカ共産党は、包括的なスパイ活動を実施する中で、ベトナム戦争を逃れるために、米兵をロシア経由でスウェーデンに脱走させる手助けをしたり、在日米軍基地に核兵器を持ち込んでいる証拠を探したりしていました。

They also wanted to use the anti-Vietnam war movement in the US, to force America to withdraw US troops from South Korea. Then North Korea would have a chance to attack the South with no US allies.

　彼らは、米国のベトナム反戦運動を利用して、韓国から米軍を撤退させる活動も行っていました。それが成功すれば、米軍の後ろ盾がなくなった韓国を、北朝鮮が攻撃しやすくなります。

I, therefore, can say that I fought in the Second Korean War. No, it never happened. But there were people who were trying to make it happen. And what I did at that time was dangerous. But I did my duty. And sometimes I experienced firsthand secret cooperation between Japan and South Korea in that world of espionage.

ですので、私は第二次朝鮮戦争を戦っていた、と言えます。まあ、その戦争は現実に起こりませんでしたが、その戦争を起こすために活動している人たちがいたのです。そして、当時の私の任務は危険を伴いましたが、私は自分の義務を果たしました。私は、諜報の世界で日韓が秘密裏に協力しているのをこの目で見てきました。

It was a shadow war, and I am grateful that it never became a real war. But I came to admire Korean people. They are very tough and hard working. I did notice that people were a bit obsessed with proving themselves better than Japan, and always comparing themselves with Japanese people.

それは影の戦争でした。現実の戦争にならなかったのは嬉しいことです。でも、その時私は韓国人を尊敬するようになりました。とても凛々しく、勤勉でした。自分たちが日本より上であることを証明することにやや取り憑かれ、いつも日本人と比較している姿をよく見ました。

After my time in the Marines, I lived in South Korea for about a year. I noticed that Koreans did not have much contact with other countries. I hoped that such contact would help them to become more sophisticated, and grow out of this obsession with Japan.

私は海兵隊の任期が終わってから、一年くらい韓国に住んでいると、韓国人は他国とはあまり付き合いがないことに気付きました。私は、韓国が外国と関わる機会が増えれば、韓国はもっと洗練された国になり、日本に執着しなくなるのではないかと期待しました。

It was a vain hope. Their obsession with Japan has twisted their National Soul.

残念ながら無理でした。韓国の日本に対する執念は、民族の性質をねじ曲げました。

Korea should learn from Vietnam
韓国はベトナムに学べ

I am not fooled by histrionic Comfort Women performances, sometimes using a wheelchair, sometimes walking. I am not some naive Westerner.

私は、時に車いすを使い、時に歩く元慰安婦の芝居じみたパフォーマンスに騙されません。私はそんなに愚直な西洋人ではありません。

All their hysterics about being a Pacific War victim do not impress me at all. I know the truth. In the Pacific War, Korea was a backwater, and there were one or two American air raids on Seoul to my memory. That is all.

大東亜戦争の犠牲者だというヒステリーは、私に何の影響も与えません。私は真実を知っています。大東亜戦争当時、朝鮮は戦争の直接的影響がほとんどない隔絶された地域で、私が記憶する限りでは、一回か二回米軍によるソウルへの空襲がありましたが、その程度でした。

Though Japan invested much in that country in 35 years of annexation, Japan never showed a profit.

日本は35年の併合時代に、朝鮮に莫大な投資をしましたが、利益にはなりませんでした。

And Japan still continues to invest in Korea today. Since the end of the Korean War, Japan has invested in everything from small-scale industries, hospitals, steel factories to dams, expressways, etc.

そして今も、日本は韓国に投資を続けています。朝鮮戦争が停戦すると、日本は小規模工業、病院、製鉄所、ダム、高速道路など、様々な分野に投資しました。

How do Korean people show their gratitude to Japan? Aren't they only going around the world, screaming about how Japan has not properly apologized for fictional bad deeds supposedly done during the war, and demanding that Japan should apologize?

それに対して、韓国人は日本に感謝の意を表していますか？　日本が戦争中にしたと想像される架空の悪行について如何に日本が適正に謝罪していないかを世界中を廻って叫び、謝罪しろと要求しているだけではないですか。

It is contrary to reason.

それは道理に反しています。

Koreans keep saying that Japan should learn from Germany, because Germany has truly apologized for what they did in WWII. Well, I am of German aristocratic blood, so I know the story well.

韓国人は、日本に対してよく「ドイツに学びなさい！」と言います。ドイツは第二次世界大戦を心から謝罪している、からだそうです。まあ、私はアメリカ生まれですが、祖先はドイツの貴族なので、ドイツのことはよく分かってます。

But I will tell Korean people that they should learn from Vietnam. In the Vietnam War, America devastated that country. America dropped more tonnage of bombs on Vietnam than on both Europe and Asia in WWII. For me, the defoliant weapons dropped were particularly terrible.

しかし、私は韓国人にこう言います。「ベトナムから学びなさい」。ベトナム戦争でアメリカはベトナムを荒廃させました。アメリカは、第二次世界大戦でヨーロッパとアジアに落とした爆弾より多くの爆弾を、ベトナムに落としました。私にとって、枯れ葉剤は特に恐ろしくひどいものでした。

South Korea sent a total of some 320,000 troops to Vietnam, and helped burn that country to the ground.

韓国は、ベトナムに約320,000人もの兵隊を派遣し、アメリカのベトナム焦土化作戦に協力しました。

I also was a US Marine, so I know that story well.

私も元米海兵隊でしたので、その戦争のことをよく知っています。

But today, the Vietnamese do not cry about being victims. They do not roam all the countries of the world, saying how awful America is. They do not demand money from anybody.

しかし、今日、ベトナム人は、自分たちは犠牲者だと叫んだりしません。世界中を巡って、アメリカはひどい国だと言いふらすようなことはしません。他国にお金を要求したりしません。

They are not like Koreans. Whenever Japanese meet Koreans in a social situation in any outside country, the Koreans always scream, "Do you know what Japan did to my country!?!?" Meanwhile, Vietnamese people never say to me, just because I was born in America, "Do you know what America did to my country?" Even though really most Americans today don't know what America did in Vietnam, such is the case.

彼らは韓国人と違います。他国の公的な場で日本人と韓国人が一緒になると、韓国人は「日本は私の国に何をしたか知っていますか？」と叫びます。一方、ベトナム人は、私がアメリカ生まれだからと言って、「アメリカが私の国に何をしたか知っていますか？」とは決して言いません。まあ、現在の大抵のアメリカ人が、アメリカが何をしたかを知らないとしても、それが事実です。

And their experience is not made up and fictional like the Korean claims are. Peoples all over the world could all see it on television.

しかも、ベトナム人の体験は韓国人の言うような作り話ではありません。世界中の人々がテレビでベトナム戦争を見ていました。

What the Vietnamese are doing now is trying to join a trade pact with Japan and America. They look to the future. The past cannot be changed, the Vietnamese are not obsessed with the past. They are a great people.

Yi Un, the last Crown Prince of Korea, a Japanese Imperial Army Lieutenant General.

李垠。大韓帝国最後の皇太子。妃は梨本宮守正王第一女子方子。大日本帝国陸軍中将。二・二六事件では鎮圧部隊を直卒。

現在のベトナム人は、日本やアメリカと貿易協定を結ぼうと努力しています。彼らは未来に目を向けています。過去は変えられませんから、ベトナム人は過去に囚われていません。素晴らしい国民です。

In the Pacific War, the Korean people fought as Japanese, as able and willing soldiers under the Empire. The Korean Crown Prince Yi Un, held the rank of Lieutenant General in the Imperial Japanese Army. He eventually commanded the 1st Air Army of the Imperial Army Air force, which defended the Japanese Home Islands.

大東亜戦争では、当時の朝鮮人は日本人として、帝国の有能で戦う意志もある兵士として戦いました。李氏朝鮮の李垠皇太子は、日本陸軍の中将になって、日本本土防空の任に当たる帝国陸軍航空部隊第一飛行軍を指揮しました。

It was after the war that Koreans made up the story that they were victims, and roamed the world begging someone to punish Japan for them.

戦後になり、韓国人は、自分たちは犠牲者であるという話を作り、日本を叩くよう世界中で触れ回っています。

What the Korean people should do is to learn a lesson from Vietnam.

韓国人がすべきことは、ベトナムから学ぶことです。

Korea's great tragedy was the Korean War, and it was a war of

South Koreans against North Koreans, not against Japan.

　韓国の最大の悲劇は朝鮮戦争でした、日本との戦争ではなく、韓国人と北朝鮮人の戦争でした。

Without Japan, South Korea would wither. It is time for South Korea to grow up.

　日本なしでは、韓国は衰退します。韓国は大人の国になる時です。

Chapter 7
Misconceptions
思い違い

Naive peaceniks and their masochistic view of history
平和ボケと自虐史観

There is a phrase in Japan called “Heiwa Boke”. It means a person so befuddled by a peaceful life that he cannot discern reality.

日本語に「平和ボケ」というフレーズがあります。平和な生活で惑わされて、現実が見えないという意味です。

One of the great problems of Japanese society today consists in Article 9 of the Japanese constitution. There is a custom of regarding written documents as sacrosanct in Asian societies, as something that cannot ever be changed.

現在の日本社会の大きな問題は、憲法第９条です。アジアの国には、書面となった文書は神聖で、侵してはならないという考えがあります。

There is another aspect, that of willingly giving way to others. In Japanese we can call this “Enryo suru”, or maybe even “Jigyaku”.

また、他人に進んで譲歩するという側面のこともあります。日本語では、これを「遠慮する」、あるいは、ことによったら「自虐」とさえ言います。

"Enryo suru" means to give way to, and to give priority to the feelings, wants and needs of others over one's own needs. "Jigyaku" means to abase oneself or something like prostrating oneself before others.

「遠慮する」というのは、譲歩し、他人の気持ち、欲しがるもの、必要とすることを、自分が必要とすることより優先することです。「自虐」の方は、自分を卑下する、他人の前にひれ伏すことです。

There is also a tendency to believe the accusations of other people or authority when someone accuses your own family of wrong doing.

　それと、自分の家族が悪いことをしたと訴えられた時、他人や当局の告発を信じてしまう傾向があります。

These traits help to make Japan a wonderful harmonious society to live in. But they are a disaster when dealing with foreigners. And particularly to Americans, living in a self- orientated society, these traits will be nearly incomprehensible.

　このような習性は、日本を住むには素晴らしく調和的な社会の形成に役立ちます。しかし、外国人と付き合う場合には、やっかいな問題を引き起こします。特に、アメリカ人は、自分優先の社会に住んでいるので、こういう特性をほとんど理解できないでしょう。

Even today, many Japanese people still do not understand foreign people at all, and they are likely to assume that foreigners will behave the same way as Japanese people do. No, never.

現在でも、数多くの日本人が、外国人を全く理解していませんし、外国人も日本人と同じように行動すると考えがちですが、決してそんなことはありません。

Article 9 is the provision in the Japanese constitution that Japan will never maintain a military or possess the weapons of war.

第９条は日本国憲法の条項で、日本は永遠に軍隊を持たない、武器を持たないというものです。

Many Japanese people still believe that this is the reason that Japan has had peace for the last 71 years. Or they truly believe that America really protects Japan. No.

数多くの日本人は、憲法のおかげで日本は71年間平和が続いてきたと信じています。または、アメリカが実際に日本を守ると心から信じています。違います。

America will only protect Japan if it is in the American interest to do so. There are two reasons for the presence of American military forces in Japan.

アメリカが日本を守るのは、アメリカの国益になる場合だけです。日本にアメリカ軍が存在している理由は二つあります。

One is to prevent Japan from becoming an independent powerful nation again. The other is to send US forces around the world. For American deployments in about half the globe, Japan is the strategic rear.

一つ目の理由は、日本が再び強い独立国にならないようにするためです。二つ目の理由は、米軍を世界中に派遣するためです。日本は地球の半分をカバーするための、重要な後方拠点です。

America still fears Japan. Well, they fear everybody and everything. America, therefore, still keeps a constant barrage of propaganda about how awful Japan was in the Pacific War.

アメリカは今でも日本を恐れています。まあ、彼らは誰にでも、何に対しても、恐れています。それで、アメリカは今もなお、大東亜戦争で日本がいかにひどいことをしたか、というプロパガンダを続けています。

The true meaning of Article 9 is that at the end of the Pacific War, Americans looked at Japanese people and saw them as lesser beings, Japanese could not be trusted to have weapons like white Christian nations.

第９条の本当の意味は、大東亜戦争が終わった時、アメリカ人は日本人が劣位の存在であると考えたということです。アメリカ人は日本人を信用できず、白人キリスト教国のように武装させたくありませんでした。

Considering how many awful and bloody wars white Christian countries conducted, this is very arrogant and condescending thinking.

白人キリスト教国が行った残虐で、血なまぐさい数多くの戦争を考えると、これはとても傲慢で、見下した考え方です。

And many Japanese continue to believe that Japan was evil in the war.

しかし、今も大多数の日本人が、日本は戦争で悪いことをしたと信じています。

I have heard all kinds of opinions from people. For example, if another country attacked Japan, we should surrender or run away. I have even read about one person who said that we should let an invader kill us all without resistance. That way, foreigners would admire Japanese people as a people of peace.

いろんな人からいろんな意見を聞きました。たとえば、外国が日本を攻撃した場合は、逃げれば良い、あるいは、すぐに降伏すれば良いと言います。またある人は、日本が侵略された場合、抵抗しないで皆殺しにされても良いと話している人のことを読んだことさえあります。そうすれば、他国から、日本は平和を愛する国だったと称賛されるということでした。

Really? If Japan were invaded, would this person gather his wife and children together and say "Let us go and get killed by the invaders, because we are peaceful." Would his family really accompany him?

本気なのでしょうか？　日本が侵略された場合、この人物が奥さんと子供たちを集めて、「私たちは平和を愛する国民なので、侵略者に殺してもらいましょう」と言うのでしょうか？　家族は本当に彼についていきますか？

These people are usually of a Leftist political bent, and very kind and nice. But seriously naive and misinformed. And foreigners would not look at Japan in admiration, but they would remark how stupid Japanese were for not fighting back.

　こういう人はだいたい政治的には左で、優しい人です。しかし、とても甘い考えで、間違っています。そしてこの場合、外国人は、日本を称賛するのではなく、抵抗しなかった日本人が如何に愚かだったかと言うでしょう。

Another reason for this "Japan-was-bad" propaganda is so that Japanese people will not look too closely into American conduct in the war. Of course, in war, bad things happen, soldiers kill. But despite what foreigners say, the Imperial Japanese forces were not brutal, and in the main conducted themselves with dignity towards civilians.

　この、日本は悪だったというプロパガンダを行うもう一つの理由は、日本人が、その戦争でのアメリカの行為をしっかり見ないようにするためです。もちろん戦争で悪いことは起こりますし、兵士は人を殺します。しかし、外国人がどう言おうとも、日本軍は残虐ではなく、基本的に一般人に対して威厳ある態度をとっていました。

On the other hand, with such things as strategic bombing, America attempted extinction of the Japanese race. There are still many Americans today who desire this.

一方、アメリカは戦略爆撃のような手段で日本国民の絶滅を試みました。今も、多くのアメリカ人がこれを望んでいます。

But so many Japanese cling to the idea that if Japan does not participate in war or defend itself, war will not happen by some miracle. They do not understand reality.

それなのに、多くの日本人は、日本が参戦も自衛もしなければ、奇跡によって戦争は起きないという考えに執着しています。彼らは、現実を理解していません。

In Chapter 1, I wrote how in Japan's mediaeval wars the common people were not involved. Thus, they do not understand how war is practiced in the rest of the world.

第1章で、日本の戦国時代では民衆は戦争に巻き込まれなかったと書きました。それで、日本人は日本以外の諸国では戦争がどのように行なわれるのか分かっていないのです。

In the rest of the world, war is about genocide. It is tribe against tribe. It means that our people will kill all of your people, take your land, exterminate your race and culture.

世界の他の国々では、戦争とは、およそ大虐殺のことです。部族対部族です。自国民が相手国民を皆殺しにして、相手国の領土を奪い、相手国民とその文化を抹殺する、ということです。

And if a country says that they love peace and will not fight back, the other country will joyfully massacre them.

もしどこかの国が、我々は平和を愛しているので全く抵抗しません、と言えば、攻撃する国は喜んで皆殺しにします。

By being militarily weak, you invite invasion by others. It is because Japan was weak after the Pacific War that South Korea landed on Takeshima, Japanese territory. They would not have attempted such an action if Japan had been strong. They captured Japanese fishing boats operating near the island, arrested many Japanese fishermen, and some were killed. The fishermen were only released after Japan released many Korean criminals from Japanese jails.

軍事的に弱い国は他国から侵略されます。韓国が日本領の竹島に上陸したのは、大東亜戦争後、日本が弱まったためです。もしその時、日本が軍事的に強い国だったら、韓国はそんなことはしなかったでしょう。竹島の近くで漁をしていた日本の漁船が拿捕され、大勢の漁民が抑留されました。死者も出ています。韓国の要求で、漁師の返還と引き換えに、日本の刑務所から韓国人の犯罪者が大勢釈放されました。

Such Japanese people as worship Article 9 think that Japan was indeed evil, and that if a war happened again, they should immediately surrender. Actually, Japan was lucky after the end of the war. Firstly, America basically took charge of the occupation. And secondly, General MacArthur led it.

第9条を崇拝している日本人は、かつての日本は本当に悪だった、もし戦争が再び起きたらすぐ降伏するべきだと思っています。実際のところ、終戦後の日本は運が良かったのです。その理由の一つ目は、日本を占領したのがアメリカだったことです。二つ目は、マッカーサー将軍がその占領の責任者だったことです。

There were other American officers who, if they had been in charge, would have taken a much more vengeful approach. For example, there were proposals to destroy all Japanese industrial capability, and make Japan an agricultural nation subordinate to America.

もし責任者になっていたら、はるかにもっと報復的な行動をとったかもしれない他のアメリカの将官たちがいました。たとえば、日本の産業を完全に潰し、日本をアメリカに従属する農業国にするという話もありました。

As of June of 1953, the Japanese government held Takeshima Island under its control and had a pillar marking its sovereignty on the island.

現在韓国に不法占拠されている竹島は、昭和 28 年 6 月の時点では行政区域標柱が設置され、日本が管理していた。

America did and still does in the present, attempt to convert Japan culturally into another version of America. But the postwar occupation was not as bad as it could have been if another country had been in charge.

　昔も、今も、アメリカは日本を文化的に小アメリカにしようとしたし、しています。それにしても、他国が担当した場合の想定に比し、戦後の占領はそれほど悪いものではありませんでした。

I have also read comments by some other Japanese people that Japan should surrender even if attacked, and they should not do anything bad to others.

　他国から攻撃された場合、日本は降伏すべきで、他国に悪いことをしてはいけないとの他の日本人の言説を読んだこともあります。

Well, war is indeed evil. But sometimes, to protect your nation and family it is necessary. There is no way to escape this fact. Some people in Japan are incredibly naive on this issue. I have met and talked with such people. They are always very nice and kind. I consider many of them to be friends.

　戦争は本当に凶悪です。でも、自分の国と家族を守るために、戦うことが必要な時もあります。この現実を避けることはできません。この問題について、本当に考えが甘すぎる日本人がいます。そういう人と話したことがありますが、本当に優しい人たちです。そういった人たちの多くが私の友人であると考えています。

But they just cannot understand that other countries think differently than Japanese people, and will act differently.

しかし、彼らが理解できないのは、他国の人は日本人とは考えが違うし、行動も違うということです。

There is one more reason for the so-called "peace Constitution" . It is that the Japanese military was so powerful that it terrified the Americans. Japan is a very small country that in a very short time went from nothing to a major military and industrial power.

この「平和憲法」なるものが存在するもう一つの理由があります。それは、日本軍が強かったため、アメリカ人が日本を恐れたことです。日本は小さく、狭い国で、何もない所から、短期間のうちに軍事的、産業的に大国になりました。

And on the whole, the Japanese population is more intelligent and certainly more hard- working than Americans. Americans do not sleep at night when they think of this, as they are terrified. They, therefore, wish to keep Japan subservient.

基本的にアメリカ人より日本人の方が賢く、一生懸命に働きます。アメリカ人がこの事実を考えると、夜も眠れなくなります。日本を怖がっているためです。だから日本を従属状態にしておきたいのです。

Americans have to let the Pacific War go. They always keep repeating endlessly the same propaganda from that time.

アメリカ人は、大東亜戦争を手放すことが必要です。その当時から、同じプロパガンダを延々と繰り返しています。

Every August, we go through the same media circus ritual. Will a Japanese Cabinet Minister visit Yasukuni shrine? Has Japan properly apologized for the war? American mass media every year bring this up.

毎年8月になると、恒例のメディアのバカ騒ぎがあります。日本の内閣総理大臣は靖国神社を参拝するのか？　日本は過去の戦争をきちんと謝罪しているのか？　アメリカのマスコミは毎年この問題を話題にします。

Well, Americans have not stopped forgiving themselves for their own Civil War of 150 years ago.

まあ、アメリカ人は150年前の南北戦争もまだ許していませんが。

But this constant nagging about Japan and the war is beginning to damage the Japanese- American relationship.

でも、この執拗なあら探しのような日本批判は、徐々に日米関係に傷をつけています。

American misconceptions about the Japanese-Korean governmental agreement
日韓合意についてのアメリカの誤解

The recent Japanese-Korean governmental agreement in

December of 2015 about the Comfort Women is a case in point.

最近の話では、2015年12月の日韓合意を見るとよく分かります。

American government sources are boasting about success in a government-to-government agreement that cannot be reversed. This is ridiculous. In a democracy, any future government has the right to say the actions of previous governments were wrong, hence the change was required.

アメリカ政府筋は、政府間での不可逆的な合意ができたことを自慢しています。これは愚かなことです。民主主義の場合、将来の政権は、過去の政権が過ちを犯したので、政権交代が起きたのだと言う権利があります。

The US government should not attempt to regulate how other countries view each other's history. America will only make enemies of everybody. I think that the Obama administration feared that the dispute between Japan and Korea would weaken American influence in eastern Asia.

アメリカ政府は、他国間の歴史認識問題に首を突っ込まない方が良いです。このままでは、アメリカは皆の敵になるだけです。私の考えでは、オバマ政権は、この日韓の歴史問題によって、東アジアでのアメリカの影響力が弱まるかもしれないという不安があったのだと思います。

Let me tell you a secret. This agreement has weakened American influence in eastern Asia. There is a lot of anti-American feeling in South Korea, I have witnessed it. The attack on ambassador Lippert in 2015 was unsuccessful, but Koreans did succeed in killing American diplomat Stevens in 1908.

一つお教えしましょう。この合意により、東アジアでのアメリカの影響力は弱まりました。韓国は反米感情が強いです。私はそれを目の当たりにしました。2015年、韓国人はリッパート米大使暗殺に失敗しましたが、1908年にはスティーブンス米外交官暗殺に成功しています。

No Japanese has ever killed a US ambassador.

アメリカ大使を殺した日本人はいません。

American advisor to the Korean Foreign Office Durham White Stevens (left) and Marquis Ito Hirobumi, both assassinated by Koreans.

韓国外交顧問米人ダーハム・ホワイト・スティーブンス（左）と侯爵伊藤博文。スティーブンスは1908年、サンフランシスコで朝鮮人に射殺された。翌年、伊藤もハルビンで朝鮮人に射殺されている。

And here is an example of what I meant when I began this chapter. To people outside Japan, since the Japanese government offered an apology for the Comfort Women issue, it probably appeared that Japan was truly evil and awful during the war.

そして、この合意は私がこの章で言いたかったことを示している一つの例です。日本以外の国の人たちは、日本政府が慰安婦問題で謝罪をしたので、日本は本当に戦争の時にひどいことをしていたのだと受け止めたでしょう。

But apologies do not mean that in Japan. In Japan it is common to offer an apology even when one did nothing wrong. It gives the other person face, and preserves peace.

しかし、日本では謝罪はそういう意味ではありません。日本では、何も悪いことをしてなくても、謝ることはよくあります。そうすることで、相手の面子を立て、良好な関係を保ちます。

I have seen so many Westerners, particularly Americans, fail to understand this concept, and leave Japan after a few years frustrated and angry. They did not succeed in their venture in Japan, because they failed to understand how Japanese communicated apologies.

私が日本に住んでから、数多くの西洋人、特にアメリカ人がこのことを理解できないで数年で、不満と怒りで日本から出ていくのを見てきました。彼らが日本での事業に失敗したのは、日本人の謝罪の仕方を理解できないからでした。

Of course, the Japanese government erred in their understanding of how foreigners would perceive this. What the Japanese government and the American government hoped to achieve was to put an end to the rancor coming from South Korea.

もちろん、外国人がこの謝罪行為をどう解釈するかということを、日本政府は見誤りました。日本政府、アメリカ政府は、韓国人が日本に対して深い恨みを持つのをやめることを望んでいました。

What both the Japanese and American governments did not understand here is that the South Koreans cannot be satisfied irrespective of how much compensation or money may be paid. They see the present existence of Japan as an insult. They wish to force Japanese subjugation to Korea, and have Japan support Korea forever, as a nation ruled and dominated by Korea.

日本政府やアメリカ政府が分かっていないのは、いくら補償金を渡したところで韓国人は満足しないということです。彼らは日本の存在が許せないのです。彼らが望んでいるのは、日本を韓国に服従させ、韓国に統治、支配される国として日本が永久に韓国を後援することなのです。

They cannot let go of that old Confucian thinking, that Korea is superior to Japan because of Confucian scholarship, and geographical proximity to China.

儒教に造詣が深く、地理的に中国に近いことから、韓国が日本より上位の存在であるという古い儒教的考えを彼らは手放すことができません。

This is not going to work out well. In South Korea, when the governmental spokesman announced that Japan would begin to pay money for the Comfort Women issue, a riot ensued. And now South Korean groups are demanding more apologies and compensation for other wartime issues, such as ethnic Koreans who were brought to Japan to forcibly work in industry.

これでは、問題解決にはなりません。韓国で、政府の報道官がこれから慰安婦問題で日本がお金を支払うことを発表したら、暴動が起きました。そして今や、韓国の団体は他の戦時の問題、たとえば朝鮮人が日本に送られ強制労働させられた等で、新たな謝罪と賠償を要求しています。

All Japanese were mobilized to work in the war, and Koreans were Japanese at the time. Again, if the labor draft had been so arduous, why did it not spark armed revolt in Korea? At that time, there was no significant Japanese military garrison in Korea, and the majority of the police were ethnic Koreans.

大東亜戦争で日本国民は皆が労働のために動員されましたが、当時朝鮮人も日本国民でした。もしこの動員がひどいものであったならば、どうして当時の朝鮮で、武装蜂起が起こらなかったのでしょうか？ 当時、朝鮮半島の日本軍の守備隊はわずかでしたし、警察官の大多数は朝鮮人でした。

With this anti-Japanese hatred that the South Korean government has stoked over the years, they have created a monster that they cannot control. The reason that they let it get so out of hand was that they overused the anti-Japan feeling to distract people from mistakes by the South Korean government.

長年にわたって、韓国政府がこの反日感情の火を煽り続けたことで、制御不能の怪物を育て上げてしまいました。怪物がこれほど大きくなってしまった原因は、韓国政府がその失政から韓国人の目をそらすために、反日を利用し過ぎたことでした。

But I think they are now afraid of what they have created.

しかし、韓国政府にとって、今や自分が育てたこの怪物が恐ろしい存在になってしまったと考えられます。

In Japan, this recent Comfort Women agreement has created resentment among an overwhelming number of Japanese people. On this issue, the Japanese Left and the Japanese Right are on the same page.

日本では、この慰安婦問題の合意は圧倒的多数の人が憤慨しています。この問題に関しては、日本の右も左も同じ意見です。

And there is growing resentment at the role of America here. Of course, for certain I do not know how much pressure America applied, or in what manner.

それから、当地では、この問題での、アメリカの役割に対しても大きな憤りがあります。もちろん、本当のところ、アメリカがどれほどの外圧をかけたのかも、どんな方法で外圧をかけたのかも、私には分かりません。

But I do read certain things written by some influential Americans, and on occasion, I meet influential Americans.

しかし、私は影響力があるアメリカ人の書いたものをよく読みますし、有力なアメリカ人と時折会うこともあります。

I am very sorry, but I have never read comments by a powerful American that show that they really understand Japan. Very few speak Japanese, and they only associate with Japanese who specialize in dealing with foreigners.

残念ながら、私はそんなアメリカ人の意見で、本当に日本を理解していると分かるものを読んだことがありません。日本語ができる人はとても少なく、外国人と関わるのが専門の日本人としか会わないのです。

They do not associate with “the Japanese man on the street”. The thing is, for example, that Japanese who specialize in dealing with foreigners, such as many Japanese business people, may say things to please foreigners, and may not necessarily say how things truly are. They have to go find that themselves.

彼らは、普通の日本人と付き合うことはありません。問題は、外国人と関わるのが専門の日本人、たとえば多くのビジネスマンなら相手の外国人を喜ばせることを言っても、真実を言わないのかもしれません。自分でその真実を見いだす必要があります。

And by this action, this Comfort Women agreement, we can plainly see that Americans do not understand the true reasons for the problems between Japan and South Korea.

この慰安婦合意によって、アメリカ人は日韓問題の本当の理由を分かっていないということがよく見えてきます。

It was a serious mistake for America to attempt to regulate historical issues between Japan and South Korea. Japanese are disappointed in America.

アメリカが日韓の間の歴史問題を統御しようとしたのは大きな間違いでした。日本人はアメリカに失望しています。

Blindfolded Americans
目隠しされているアメリカ人

Also, Americans have to let the historical anger go. Pearl Harbor Day always being celebrated in America is beginning to rankle in Japan. Frankly, even when I was a child in America, I could not get angry about the Pearl Harbor attack. OK, the Japanese Navy attacked the American Navy, there was a hard war, and a few years later eventually America won. So what?

それから、アメリカ人は歴史問題で怒ることをやめなければなりません。真珠湾攻撃の日に特別な儀式を行い続けていますが、それが日本人をいらつかせ始めています。正直に言うと、私はアメリカに住んでいた子供の時、真珠湾攻撃に対して怒りを覚えることができませんでした。日本海軍がアメリカ海軍を攻撃し、激戦が続き、数年後にアメリカが勝った、それだけの話ではないですか。

But Americans make it some kind of religion that evil Japan did some great wrong by sneakily attacking righteous America. Well, we have the American concept of exceptionalism here. Americans think that they are the most perfect nation, and that they can do no wrong.

しかし、アメリカ人は悪の日本が正義のアメリカを騙し討ちしたことを、ある種の信仰にしています。これはアメリカ例外主義の考え方です。アメリカ人は、自分たちが世界で最も優れた理想の国であると信じています。自分の国は悪いことはしないと信じています。

I remember that in 2003 President Bush started an air raid and invasion of Iraq with no declaration of war. So why do Americans still, 75 years after the Pearl Harbor attack, call it a sneak attack? Why do they not call their 2003 invasion of Iraq a sneak attack? Why do they still demonize Japan?

2003年にブッシュ大統領が宣戦布告をしないでイラクを空襲、侵略を開始したことを覚えています。それなのに、なぜ、真珠湾攻撃から75年も経っているのに、今も騙し討ちと言えるのでしょうか？　なぜ自分たちのイラクへの侵略は騙し討ちと呼ばないのでしょうか？　なぜ日本だけを悪者扱いするのでしょうか？

Since Americans wear blinders, they cannot imagine doing any wrong. Always the other country is wrong in their understanding. Concerning Japan, they cling to the propaganda that after the Pacific War, America recreated evil Japan into a good nation.

アメリカ人は視野が狭くて、アメリカが悪いことをしたということが想像できません。いつも、相手の国が悪いと考えます。大東亜戦争後、アメリカが悪の日本を良い国に作り直したというプロパガンダにしがみついています。

But America has to stop thinking like this, since it is causing resentment in Japan.

しかし、アメリカはこんな考え方はやめた方が良いでしょう、日本では反感を買っています。

And with the history issues, too many Americans make judgement on prewar Japan based on social concepts in the United States today. The Comfort Women issue is a serious example. Many Americans assume that any kind of prostitution is a form of sexual slavery.

Row of American battleships on fire during the Pearl Harbor attack by Japanese naval task force.

日本機動部隊の真珠湾攻撃を受け、炎上する米戦艦群。

歴史問題では、戦前の日本について、現在のアメリカ社会を価値基準にして判断しているアメリカ人が多過ぎます。慰安婦問題は深刻な事例です。多くのアメリカ人は、どんな状況下での売春も性奴隷だと見なします。

But Asians look at it in a much different way. In any case, it is not correct for the American government to be used by some Americans to punish Japan for what it was 70 years ago, but no longer is.

しかし、アジア人の考え方はまるで違います。とにかく、一部のアメリカ人が、米政府を利用して70年前のことで現在はそうでないことで日本を罰しようとするのは、正しいことではありません。

If you want to combat prostitution, why not do something about those thousands of Korean girls trafficked into the US every year?

もしアメリカ人が売春問題を何とかしたいのなら、どうして毎年、人身売買されてアメリカに連れて来られる何千人もの韓国人女性のために活動しないのですか？

The enduring hatred of the American Civil War
いまだにくすぶる南北戦争の遺恨

I have my doubts if Americans can put aside history. Even now, Americans are still fighting about what happened in the American Civil War of 1861 to 1865.

私は、アメリカ人が歴史を忘れることができるかどうか怪しいと思っています。というのも、現在でも、アメリカ人は1861年から1865年の南北戦争での事象のことで争っています。

In 2015 there was a big outcry over the use of Confederate symbols in the US. For example, some State flags in the South still had the Confederate battle flag, the Stars and Bars, included in their design.

2015年にアメリカで、旧南部連合国のシンボルの使用について大論争がありました。たとえば、アメリカのいくつかの南部の州がまだアメリカ連合国の国旗「スターズ・アンド・バーズ」を、その州旗のデザインに含んでいました。

Many people in the North cried out that this showed that the South was unrepentant and that there was still prejudice against black people.

これに対し、北部の数多くのアメリカ人は、これは南部が戦争を反省していないことを示しており、黒人差別意識の現れであると訴えたのです。

So that is the reason that Americans today criticize Japan about Yasukuni shrine, Pearl Harbor and Comfort Women. If they cannot forgive other Americans, and worry about another war over issues of 150 years ago, how can they ever forget a war of 70 years ago with Japan?

これは、現在のアメリカ人が靖国神社、真珠湾攻撃、慰安婦問題で日本を批判をしているのと同じ理由です。他のアメリカ人を許せず、150年前の事実を巡るアメリカ人同士の戦争の心配をしているのに、70年前の日本人との戦争を忘れることができるでしょうか？

And virtually no Americans understand the true causes of the American Civil War. Just as Americans today do not understand that America provoked the attack on Pearl Harbor.

そして、南北戦争の本当の原因を分かっているアメリカ人はほとんどいません。同じように、アメリカが日本を真珠湾攻撃に追い込んだという事実も知りません。

For those Japanese people who think unarmed pacifism is a good thing, let us take a quick look at the American Civil War. The South and North were very different in culture, and many problems, including the issue of slavery, led the South to declare independence and secede from the Union.

非武装の平和主義が良いことだと考えている日本人のために、ちょっと南北戦争のことをお話ししましょう。当時のアメリカは南部と北部でまるで文化が違い、様々な問題がありました。奴隷制もその中の一つでした。そんな様々な問題が原因で南部がアメリカ合衆国からの独立を宣言し、アメリカ連合国から離脱しました。

The Union could not abide this, mobilized an army and attacked the South. The South simply wanted to become independent and be left alone without contact with the North.

北部はこのことを許せず、軍隊を動員し南部を攻撃しました。南部はただ独立して北部と関わりを持たないことを望んでいただけでした。

Today, Northerners think that the Civil War was a humanitarian effort to free slaves, but that is not true. At the time, most Northerners had no desire to free the slaves. It was not until two years into the war when he was sure that he could win the war that President Lincoln declared all slaves to be free.

現在の北部のアメリカ人は、南北戦争は奴隷を解放した人道的な活動だと思っていますが、事実は違います。当時、北部に住んでいるほとんどのアメリカ人は、そんなことは考えていませんでした。リンカーン大統領が奴隷解放宣言を行ったのは、戦争が始まって2年経ち、彼らが北部の勝利を確信できた後のことでした。

There were some 620,000 military deaths in the Civil War, which does not count civilians. When the North decided to force war and not negotiate, the choices for the South were either to surrender and suffer destruction of their society, or to fight and try to preserve their society and culture. This is the same type of choice that Japan faced under the pressure from America just before launching the Pacific War.

南北戦争では、約620,000人の兵士が死亡しました。この数に、一般人の死亡者は含まれていません。北部が交渉を拒否して、強引に戦争を開始した時に、南部の選択肢は二つでした。降伏して、自分たちの社会と文化の崩壊を受け入れるか、それとも自分たちの社会と文化を守るために戦うか、でした。これは、大東亜戦争開始直前に、日本がアメリカの圧力によって、迫られた選択肢と同じ類型のものでした。

In one famous campaign, Sherman's March to the Sea, he killed 3% of the people who died in that war. This was after the battle of Atlanta in 1864. Many Japanese people probably know this battle from the movie "Gone with the Wind".

著名な作戦の一つ、シャーマン将軍の「海への進軍」で、彼は南北戦争の全死亡者数の3%を殺しました。これは、1864年のアトランタの戦いの後に起きました。アトランタの戦いを「風と共に去りぬ」の映画で知ってる日本人も多いでしょう。

General Sherman's" March to the Sea" in the American civil War. This campaign, which needlessly destroyed all thoroughly from the railway infrastructure, and industrial facilities to personal assets, was of the same nature as the later air raids on Japan.

南北戦争におけるシャーマン将軍の「海への進軍」。鉄道などの基盤、産業施設、個人の資産に至るまで無用に徹底的に無用に破壊し尽くすこの戦略は、後の日本本土空襲と同質のものであった。

After that battle General Sherman marched south to the Atlantic coast at the city of Savannah. His army marched in a group 60 miles wide. They destroyed every town and farm they passed through. It was 5 weeks of destruction without even one battle.

その戦いの後、シャーマン将軍の軍は大西洋岸南部のサバンナまで進みました。シャーマン軍の進軍の幅は100キロメートルで、行軍中に軍が通過した街、農家など破壊の限りを尽くしました。戦闘は一度もないまま、5週間破壊を続けました。

North Korea, a master of deceit
欺瞞の達人・北朝鮮

It is not my intention here to say that Americans are exceptionally cruel and bloody. But that is the nature of war. It was to prevent this from happening in Japan that Japanese leaders fought valiantly from the Meiji Restoration until Showa era.

私は、アメリカ人が特に残酷で残忍な国民であると言いたいのではありません。しかし、戦争とはそういうものです。日本はそんな目に遭わないように、明治維新から昭和まで日本の指導者たちが勇敢に戦いました。

And one thing I will say to Americans about this Japan-Korea problem. North Korea is not a military threat. They cannot invade the South, Their missiles always crash. In any case, they do not have much nuclear material. And as the South Koreans lie about the annexation era with Japan, so do the North Koreans lie.

日韓問題について、アメリカ人に言いたいことが一つあります。北朝鮮に軍事的な危険性はありません。彼らが韓国を侵略するのは不可能です。ミサイルはいつも墜落します。いずれにしても、核物質はあまりありません。韓国人が日本の併合時代について嘘を言うのと同じように、北朝鮮人も嘘を言います。

They exaggerate their military capability. Frankly, I do not believe that they have a working nuclear weapon. I think that their nuclear tests are simply using masses of conventional explosives laced with nuclear material.

彼らは軍事力を誇張しています。率直に言うと、私は彼らが使える核兵器を持っているとは思いません。核実験は核物質を加えた通常の爆発物を大量に使用しているでしょう。

Even if everything were wonderful for them, the best they could have would be only a few nuclear weapons. America has 5,000 nuclear weapons.

仮に実験が上手くいき、本当に核兵器を製造できたとしても、せいぜい数個くらいしか造ることはできないでしょう。アメリカは5,000個の核兵器を保有しています。

To start a war with nuclear weapons would be suicide for North Korea. They are not suicidal, even though their actions are often bizarre. They are just trying to show the world that they are dangerous. They believe that they are in danger of attack from America. They make these threats to preserve their nation.

北朝鮮が核戦争を始めるのは自殺行為です。彼らはいつもおかしな行動をとっていますが、自殺的なことはやりません。世界の国々に自分たちが危険な存在であると見せたいだけです。アメリカから攻撃される危険性があると信じているので、自国を守るためにそのように威圧しているのです。

When Madeleine Albright visited North Korea as the American Secretary of State, the entire city of Pyongyang was mobilized. All military personnel, governmental workers played parts in a massive theatrical show.

マデレーン・オルブライトはアメリカ国務長官の時に、北朝鮮を訪問しました。その時、平壌市民に動員がかけられました。軍人、政府職員が、大がかりな芝居の役者を演じました。

Some people were taxi drivers, some were street vendors of fried meats, some were lined up as passengers for the bus. The streets and stores were filled with busy people, the shelves of the stores visible to the Secretary's motorcade were laden with ample goods.

タクシー運転手、焼肉の露店商人、行列してバスを待つ人などがいました。道も店も人がいっぱいで活気にあふれ、国務長官たちの車列から見える店の棚には商品がたくさん積まれていました。

All this happened on the route Secretary Albright traveled. A few blocks away to either side, the streets were deserted as normal. All was a massive show of deception.

こういったことは、オルブライト国務長官が通った道筋で起こりました。そのルートの両側数ブロック先は、いつもの寂れた通りでした。全てが大がかりな欺瞞だったのです。

The Korean people, both North and South, have this talent for deception, but the talent is not available for producing real accomplishments. Well, if you look back to the Yi dynasty Korea, before the Japanese annexation, the Yangban class dictated their own reality, and nobody could contradict them. It seems that Koreans cannot throw off the burdens of their history.

コリアの国民は、南北ともこのような欺瞞の才能がありますが、彼らの才能では、本当の成果を生むことは難しいです。まあ、朝鮮併合時代の前の李氏朝鮮時代を考えると、両班たちは自分たちの好きなように現実を動かし、両班に逆らう者はいませんでした。やはり、コリアの国民はこの歴史の足かせを外すことはできないようです。

So why worry about a military pipsqueak like North Korea? For America, South Korean bases only have strategic meaning in a war against North Korea. They are useless for projecting US power anywhere else.

なぜアメリカは北朝鮮のような軍事的に取るに足らない国を、そんなに心配するのでしょう？　アメリカにとって、戦略的に韓国にある軍事基地は北朝鮮との戦争にしか使えません。地球の他の地域にアメリカの軍事力を放出するためには役に立ちません。

What America should strive for
アメリカが目指すべきもの

But Japan is strategically vital for the US. Without the bases in Japan, America cannot fight anywhere in Asia or the Middle East.

しかし、アメリカにとって、日本は戦略的に必要不可欠です。日本の基地がなければ、アメリカはアジアの如何なる地域でも中東でも戦争ができません。

I do not agree with most American wars, and this is a fact.

私はアメリカの戦争にはほとんど賛成していませんが、これは事実です。

Also, Japanese people genuinely like Americans. I can say that all Japanese people of all political persuasions do like them. Some may not like certain American policies, but they like American people and culture.

また、日本人は、心からアメリカ人のことが好きです。どんな政治信条の人もアメリカ人が好きだと言えます。アメリカの政策が嫌いな人はいますが、それでもアメリカ人やアメリカの文化は好きです。

This was also true in 1941. America provoked Japan into attacking the US in the mistaken belief that it was China that would be America's servant in Asia.

この状況は、1941年でも当てはまりました。アメリカは中国こそがアジアでの自国の僕であるという間違った信念に立ち、日本がアメリカを攻撃するよう挑発しました。

That was a total mistake to America. If America had made a partnership with Japan then, the world would be a much better place today.

これはアメリカにとり完全な間違いでした。当時、アメリカが日本と協力的な関係を作っていたら、今の世界ははるかにもっと良い世界になっていたでしょう。

Americans should stop worrying about whether Japan may become a military state again, and instead should look at how to strengthen their partnership with Japan for the future.

アメリカ人はもう、日本が再び軍事国家になるんじゃないかと心配するのはやめて、将来のために日本との協力関係をいかに強化するか考えるべきです。

The fantasy of reunification
南北再統一の幻想

As for the Koreans, they are liable to become way too emotional for their own good.

韓国人についてですが、彼らは自分たちの利益のために感情的になり過ぎです。

What do I mean?

私が言いたいのはこういうことです。

One of the true intents of South Korean groups who keep up all this trouble about history is to join North and South Korea together, and then attack, destroy, and humiliate Japan.

日本との歴史問題で騒いでいる韓国の団体の本当の目的は、北朝鮮と韓国を統一することと、日本を攻撃し破壊し、恥をかかせることです。

In their minds, they will then create the greatest nation on earth.

そうすれば世界で最も素晴らしい国が創れると考えているようです。

There are many problems and dangers with this thinking.

この考え方には、たくさんの問題と危険性があります。

These Southern groups are in a real hurry for reunification. Well, I am an ethnic German, and I know something about this. I watched the reunification of East and West Germany with great interest.

これらの統一を願う韓国の団体はとにかく早く再統一したいと考えています。まあ、私はドイツ系なので、このことについては多少分かります。私は東西ドイツの統一を大変興味深く注視しました。

First of all, East Germany was the showplace of the Communist world. Yet only 10% of households had a telephone. The cultural and economic gap with West Germany was huge.

まず、東ドイツは共産主義世界における模範国家でした。それでも電話がある家は10%程度しかありませんでした。東と西ドイツの文化的なギャップはとても大きいものでした。

After reunification, 80% of East Germans had to find a new profession. Some of the East German military enlisted personnel and equipment, notably Mig-29 fighters were kept. But all East German military officers had to quit.

再統一後、80%の東ドイツ人は新たな職業を探す必要がありました。東ドイツ軍の一部の下士官兵と装備、注目すべきところではミグ29戦闘機がドイツ軍に残りましたが、将校は全員除隊させられました。

After reunification, politically, socially, economically, the West totally dominated the East.

再統一後、政治的にも、社会的にも、経済的にも西が東を完全に支配しました。

Even today, the Eastern part of Germany still lags behind the West economically, and Western prejudice toward Easterners still exists.

現在もドイツの東側は経済的に西側に遅れていて、西ドイツ人による東ドイツ人に対する差別が今もあります。

But there was contact to an extent between the two Germanys even in the cold war. They could send mail to each other. Phone calls could be made. West Germans could freely enter East Germany. Once East Germans reached retirement age, they could go to West Germany.

しかし、冷戦時代も東西ドイツの間で、ある程度関係が保たれていました。お互いに郵便を送ることができましたし、電話をかけることもできました。西ドイツ人は自由に東ドイツに入国することができましたし、東ドイツ人は定年に達したら、西ドイツに入ることもできました。

North and South Korea on the other hand, have had virtually no contact. The only way for a North Korean to go to South is an arduous journey through China at the risk of their lives.

それに対して、北朝鮮と韓国の間では、そんなことはほとんどありません。北朝鮮人が南へ行くには、中国を経由して命がけで困難な旅をするしか方法がありません。

In the years after the Korean War, the language of both nations has grown apart, and some 30% of each language is now unintelligible to the other.

朝鮮戦争後、次第に南北の言葉が変化したため、現在、お互いに３割程度の言葉を理解できません。

In 1904 when the Russo-Japanese War started, Yi dynasty Koreans only had to worry about Japan and Russia.

1904年の日露戦争開戦時、李氏朝鮮が懸念すべきは日本とロシアだけでした。

But now China is also a great power, and America lurks behind Japan. Reunification is so much more complicated, but Koreans are too unrealistic and emotional.

しかし今は、中国も大国になり、日本の背後にはアメリカも控えています。統一は本当に複雑で困難になっているのに、今の韓国人は現実的ではなく、感情的になり過ぎです。

A hasty reunification will definitely result in Civil War. North Korea is isolated, but I think that some things are easy to understand. When Nicolae Ceausescu, President of Romania and his wife were executed in 1989, Kim Jong-il of North Korea showed films of the event to elite North Koreans.

拙速な統一では絶対に内乱になります。北朝鮮は孤立している国ですが、解りやすい側面もあると思います。ルーマニアのニコラエ・チャウシェスク大統領が1989年に処刑された時、北朝鮮の金正日は自国のエリートたちにその処刑の映像を見せました。

He said that if they did not hold together, this would happen to them. And he was right. If we look at the unification of Germany, the prosperous West completely swallowed the East.

彼のメッセージは、北朝鮮のエリートも団結して努力しないと、このように処刑されるぞ、ということです。彼は正しかったです。ドイツの統一では、繁栄している西側が東側を完全に飲み込みました。

The gap between North and South Korea is extreme. Something like this would be bound to happen in rushed unification. The Northerners would attempt to dominate the South using the same Southern people who demonstrate about the Comfort Women and other anti-Japan issues.

北朝鮮と韓国の間にあるギャップはとても深いです。急な統一では、東西ドイツの統一のようなことが起きてしまいます。北朝鮮人は、慰安婦問題などの反日問題でデモに参加する韓国人たちを使って、韓国を支配しようとするでしょう。

Koreans would hold a dream of a united strong Korea. But they would be desperate. It would ignite a Civil War. Russia, China, Japan, and the US would all interfere, and all of them would wonder what kind of Korea would arise from this mess. They would try to ensure that it would be a Korea that reflects their respective interests.

韓国人たちは強い統一コリアという夢を抱くことでしょう。しかし、それは無謀です。その結果、内乱を招きかねません。ロシア、中国、日本、アメリカが介入してきます。この四ヵ国は、今後コリアが混乱の中からどういう国になるのかを考えることでしょう。コリアが自分たちそれぞれの国益にかなう国になるようにしようと四ヵ国は働きかけるでしょう。

This is exactly what happened toward the end of the Yi dynasty. They could not make up their mind whether to look to Russia or Japan. They maybe thought that they could play some sort of balancing game between Japan and Russia.

李氏朝鮮時代の末期も同様のことが起きました。彼らはロシアにつくか、日本につくかを決められなかったのです。日露両国の間で、何とか均衡を保ったまま存在できると思ったのかもしれません。

They had no comprehension of the outside world, and because of centuries of incompetent domestic rule and intrigue, no competent officials were developed to manage the country's affairs.

彼らは自分の国の外で起きていることを、全く理解していませんでした。それに、何世紀も続いた無能な支配と策謀で、国を運営できるような有能な人材が育っていませんでした。

The result was annexation by Japan. In this age, I do not think that that will repeat itself. In the Korean War of 1950 to 1953, a world nuclear war was avoided by the Americans and Russians agreeing to restore the status quo, a front line near the 38th parallel, the parallel which had been determined by the two countries prior to the war.

その結果、日本に併合されたのです。今の時代、それは繰り返されないでしょう。朝鮮戦争の時は、戦争前に米ソが取り決めた38度線付近に軍事境界線を戻すことで米ソが合意し、核戦争は回避されました。

But if a civil war took place and modern weapons were used, Korea would be devastated. Many would die. There would be risk of a worldwide nuclear war. I understand the desire for reunification. But they should not be emotional.

しかし今、内乱が起こって現代の兵器が使用されれば、コリアは崩壊するでしょう。数多くの人が亡くなるでしょうし、世界的な核戦争に発展する可能性もあります。統一したいという気持ちは分かりますが、感情だけで動いてはダメです。

Even if they succeeded in reunifying, it would result in the movement of people. And it would be from North to South. Infrastructure is nonexistent in the North, and they don't have electricity 24 hours a day.

再統一が成功しても、人間が移動するだけの結果となるでしょう。北から南への移動のみです。北朝鮮にはインフラはありません。1日24時間使える電気は流れていません。

Not many Southerners would want to live in the North because life there would be too primitive. Yet the Northerners who would come to the South would not comprehend what a capitalist society is, and so could not easily adapt to a competitive modern society.

北の生活は原始的過ぎて、そこに住みたいと思う南の人はあまり多くないでしょう。しかし、南へ行く北の人々は資本主義社会を理解していないので、現代の競争社会に容易に適応できません。

Since in this scenario, some sort of collapse of the North military and police would happen in the North, Northerners would come to the South well-armed. There are all sorts of arms depots for reserve forces, scattered across North Korea.

　このシナリオでは、北の軍や警察も崩壊しているので、南へ流入する人たちはしっかり武装しているでしょう。北朝鮮のあちこちに予備役のための兵器庫があります。

And they have grown up in hardship, and will be much tougher than Southerners both mentally and physically.

　それに、苦しい生活の中で育ってきたのですから、南の人より精神的にも肉体的にも強いです。

The result would be an explosion in the number of nasty criminal gangs in South Korea. This is not any kind of derogatory statement about Korean character, this is reality. Things were pretty bleak in Russia when the Soviet Union collapsed.

　その結果、韓国国内で厄介な暴力集団が急増するでしょう。これはコリアンの国民性を侮辱しようというものではなく、現実の話です。ソ連崩壊後のロシアも、とても厳しい状況になりました。

Again, in Korea there would be much social disorder and riots, and many people would die.

　そして、コリアで起こる社会的混乱、暴動で、数多くの人々が亡くなるでしょう。

Be realistic. Reunification will take decades of hard work among countries concerned. But they will need truth in education in their own country, South Korea. These anti-Japan activities must stop. They have no basis in truth. Anti-Japan education is producing Koreans who do not know their true history. They will be unable to function in the world.

現実的になってください。統一は関係各国の何十年間にもわたる協力を必要とします。しかし、そのためには韓国自身が正しい教育をしなければなりません。一連の反日活動をやめる必要があります。実際、その活動には根拠がありません。反日教育によって、自分たちの本当の歴史を知らない韓国人が大量生産されました。彼らは、世界でまともに機能できないでしょう。

Korea's true tragedy, the Korean War
コリアの本当の悲劇「朝鮮戦争」

And remember that the only country that has ever treated the Korean people with compassion, and regard for their advancement and well-being, is Japan. And by constantly funding various projects in Korea, Japan still does.

それから、これまでにコリアの国民に同情し、その発展と福祉に配慮し遇した国は日本だけであることを覚えておいてください。今も日本は韓国に対して様々な分野で資金を出すことによって、そうしています。

All countries that have had wars have had difficult times. But Japan did nothing evil to Korea, and it, I dare say, was the other way around. Japan actually made every effort to raise them up to an equal level with Japan.

戦争が経験したどの国も、厳しい時期がありました。しかし、日本は韓国に対してひどいことはしていません。むしろ逆でした。日本は実際は韓国を日本と対等なレベルに引き上げる努力をしてきました。

And all this anti-Japan education, and worldwide anti-Japan activities such as building Comfort Women statues can only hurt Koreans.

反日教育や、世界中に慰安婦像を設置するような反日活動は、韓国人にとって不利益になります。

When Koreans travel overseas, they learn that much of their education has been a lie. This will devastate people, and when they return to Korea, they are a potential revolutionary group.

韓国人が海外に旅行すると、自分の受けた教育の多くが嘘だと分かります。これは彼らを呆然とさせます。そして韓国へ帰る時には潜在的な革命グループになっています。

Here I would like to describe Korea's true tragedy, the Korean War.

以下では、コリアの本当の悲劇、朝鮮戦争について説明します。

The Soviet Russian attack into Manchuria began on August 9th,

1945. The Russian tank forces were highly skilled in armored warfare, having defeated Germany. Since Japan had no large tank units of their own, and the best units had been withdrawn from Manchuria to fight America, the Russians quickly penetrated and took major Manchurian cities.

ソ連による満洲への攻撃は1945年8月9日に始まりました。ドイツを打ち破ったソ連の機甲師団は、戦車戦に非常に熟練していました。日本軍には強力な戦車部隊がなく、さらに満洲にいた精鋭部隊が対米戦のために満洲から引き抜かれていたので、ソ連部隊は容易に侵入し、満洲の主な都市を占領しました。

Japan surrendered on August 15th, but fighting in Manchuria continued for some time. But in late August, all Japanese forces in Manchuria and northern Korea surrendered to Soviet Russian forces.

日本の降伏は8月15日でしたが、その後しばらくの間満洲での戦いが続きました。しかし、8月の終わりまでに、満洲および北部朝鮮にいた日本軍は全てソ連軍に降伏しました。

On August 18 Soviet forces made amphibious landings in northern Korea. The Russian advance stopped at the 38th parallel as agreed with America.

8月18日ソ連軍が朝鮮北部に上陸しましたが、アメリカとの合意により、ソ連軍の進攻は38度線で止まりました。

US forces landed at Inchon on September 8th 1945. But Japanese military and police units carried on their functions for maintaining order under American orders south of the 38th parallel until enough American units arrived to establish law and order. But all such Japanese forces were disarmed by the Americans within a few months after the surrender, and returned to Japan.

1945年9月8日、米軍部隊が輸送船で仁川に到着し、上陸を始めました。アメリカの部隊はまだ数が少なかったので、38度線の南側で法と秩序を確立できる米軍部隊の数が揃うまで、秩序維持のため日本の軍と警察がアメリカの指示で任務を続けていました。しかし、降伏数ヵ月後、全ての日本軍はアメリカ軍に武装解除されて、日本に帰国しました。

By the end of 1945, there were no Japanese forces whatsoever in the Korean peninsula.

1945年の終わりには、朝鮮半島に日本兵は一人もいなくなりました。

Both Soviet Russia and America established a client state on their own sides of the 38th parallel. In the North, the Russians made Kim Il-Sung, a former Soviet Army officer, leader, in the South, America chose Rhee Syngman.

アメリカとソ連は38度線の南北にそれぞれ自分の従属国を創りました。北側では元ソ連軍の士官である金日成を指導者として立て、南側ではアメリカは李承晩を選びました。

From this time on in the South there arose a serious guerrilla insurgency with some 8,000 active guerrillas. Their areas of operation were in Andong area, the Taebaek, Odae, and Chiri mountain regions.

この時から韓国内で本格的なゲリラによる反乱が始まり、約8,000人のゲリラが戦闘を開始しました。活動の地域は、安東の辺りで、太白、五台山、智異の山岳地帯でした。

In counterguerrilla operations, President Rhee killed many Koreans, and it is this wave of refugees at this time that accounts for the presence of so many ethnic Koreans in Japan to this day.

Kim Il-Sung of North Korea (above), Rhee Syngman of South Korea with General MacArthur.

若き日の金日成（上）と李承晩、マッカーサー。

ゲリラ討伐の際、李大統領が多くの韓国人を殺したので、この時発生した難民が日本に流れ、その多くが現在の在日韓国人になっています。

The story that there were forced laborers brought to Japan is another Korean falsehood, and they were refuges from South Korean repression.

労働者として日本に強制連行されてきたというのは、もう一つの韓国人の嘘です。彼らは韓国の抑圧から流れてきた難民でした。

In 1950, June 25th, the North Koreans launched a massive offensive. They had a well- trained army of over 200,000 men. The core of this army were some 40,000 ethnic Koreans who had fought with the Soviet Army in WWII, and who fought with the Chinese Communist Army in the Chinese Civil War, battle-experienced veterans.

1950年6月25日に北朝鮮が大規模な攻撃を開始しました。20万人以上の精鋭兵士がいましたが、その中心は第二次世界大戦でソ連軍と一緒に戦ったり、国共内戦で中共軍と一緒に戦ったりした約4万人の朝鮮系の実戦経験者でした。

The North Koreans also possessed 150 tanks and 130 combat aircraft.

北朝鮮軍は戦車150台と戦闘機130機も保有していました。

South Korea did not have any tanks, and only a few trainer

aircraft. One third of the men did not have a uniform. Many used Japanese rifles from Japanese depots left behind in Korea. South Korean troops fought bravely, and soldiers even tried to destroy North Korean tanks with suicide bombs.

韓国軍には戦車が１台もなく、飛行機は練習機が数機あるだけでした。三分の一の韓国兵は軍服がなく、多くの韓国兵は残っていた日本軍の倉庫の武器を使用しました。韓国軍は勇敢に戦い、兵士は北朝鮮の戦車を破壊するために、爆弾を抱えて自爆攻撃しました。

The background behind that was that America simply had not supplied enough weaponry. since they did not think South Korea to be very important.

アメリカは、韓国をそれほど重要だとは考えておらず、十分に武器を供給していませんでした。

But to no avail.

しかし、韓国軍の奮闘も無駄でした。

The North Koreans quickly advanced into Seoul, and the Korean government fled to Pusan. It was here that arrival of many American units maintained the line.

北朝鮮軍が一気にソウルを占領して、韓国政府は釜山に逃げました。釜山にアメリカ軍が続々と到着し、戦線を維持しました。

General MacArthur counterattacked by an amphibious landing at Inchon, and advanced into North Korea. Most of the North Korean army was basically cut off in the south near Pusan, they took to the mountains to conduct guerrilla warfare. The Chinese army sent massive amounts of troops into Northern Korea unnoticed by America.

マッカーサー将軍が仁川上陸作戦で反撃を開始して、北朝鮮側に進攻しました。北朝鮮軍の多くは南の釜山附近で、分断され、山に逃げ込みゲリラ戦を始めました。一方中国は、アメリカの知らぬ間に北朝鮮に大軍を送り込みました。

In a great offensive, the Chinese army drove to a line south of Seoul. Then the UN Command gradually pushed back the Chinese north to the present Demilitarized line, where fighting continued on that line for two years while negotiations were also under way.

中国軍は猛攻撃を開始して、ソウルを越えてさらに南下しましたが、国連軍の反撃を受け、徐々に今の軍事境界線附近まで押し戻され、その線で２年間、膠着した状態が続きました。その間、停戦交渉が続けられました。

America had about 5 army and 1 marine divisions, Great Britain sent a division, and Turkey sent a brigade, Thailand, Canada, and the Philippines sent regimental-sized forces. France sent a battalion, and many other countries also contributed forces including tiny Luxembourg, which sent 44 men.

アメリカはほぼ陸軍５個師団と海兵の１個師団、英国は１個師団、トルコは１個旅団を派遣しました。タイ、カナダ、フィリピンは連隊クラスの部隊を派遣し、フランスは1個大隊でした。数多くの国が兵士を派遣して、ルクセンブルクのような小さい国も44人を派遣しました。

A cease-fire was concluded in 1953, and the situation stays the same today, but it is still tense with many incidents happening. When I lived in South Korea in the late 1970s it was common that the North would send commandos into South Korea by fishing boat, and repeatedly shoot up some coastal villages until they were caught and killed.

1953年に停戦となってから現在まで同じ状態が続いています。しかし、今も緊張が続いており、多くの事件が起きている状態です。私が韓国に住んでいた1970年代には、北朝鮮が漁船で特殊部隊を韓国に送り込み、自分たちが全滅するまで銃を乱射して沿岸村を破壊するという事件がよくありました。

United Nations tanks in the Korean War.

朝鮮戦争に参戦した国連軍の戦車部隊。

Guerrilla warfare by Communists originally living in South Korea and remnants of the Northern army which invaded the South continued behind the line until 1955/1956.

最初から韓国にいた共産主義者と、韓国国内に取り残され、潜伏したままの北朝鮮軍は、1955年、1956年まで、国境線内側でゲリラ戦を展開しました。

The last North Korean guerrilla in South Korea was finally captured in 1963.

韓国にいた最後のゲリラは1963年にようやく捕まりました。

One thing here, while during the annexation period, the Japanese government was aware of Communist underground political activities in areas of South Korea, there were no Communist uprisings.

併合時代、朝鮮に共産主義の地下組織があることを日本政府は知っていました。しかし、共産党員による蜂起はありませんでした。

This was because the Korean people would not support such an underground uprising against Japanese rule. It was amid the post-Pacific War chaos that the Communist guerrillas were able to make such revolts.

朝鮮人は当時の日本統治に大きな不満はなく、反乱を支持しなかったからです。大東亜戦争後の混乱で、共産主義ゲリラにそのような反乱のチャンスが訪れたのです。

What Koreans should strive for
韓国人は何を目指すのか？

Also, foreigners are becoming tired of constant Korean complaining. And more and more foreigners are learning the truth of what happened in the war. The truth always comes out eventually. But when foreigners discover the truth about this Japanese-Korean issue, they will see Koreans as a people to be shunned.

それから、外国人は韓国人の止むことのない反日の主張にうんざりしています。外国人も大東亜戦争で何があったのか、少しずつその事実を学んできています。真実はいずれ広まるものです。しかし、外国人がこの日韓問題の真実を知ってしまうと、韓国人は世界中の人々から敬遠されるべき国民と見做されるでしょう。

Is that their goal?

韓国人はそんなことを目指しているのですか？

They must quit blaming Japan for their own shortcomings. Now it has been more than 70 years since the war ended. What keeps them from becoming a great country? Look in the mirror.

韓国人たちは、自分たちの短所を日本のせいにするのをやめるべきです。終戦から70年も経っているのに、なぜ大国になれないのでしょうか？　鏡を見てください。

Afterword
おわりに

In Chapter 5, all of the statistics come from the book "The New Korea" written by Alleyne Ireland. It is an excellent book for the scholar of Japanese-Korean annexation period, since it is full of facts about just how Japan did to raise Korea up to a comparable level of civilization with that of Japan.

第５章の統計データは全て、アレン・アイルランド著『朝鮮が劇的に豊かになった時代』から引用しました。この本は朝鮮併合時代を学ぶ者にとって素晴らしい情報源であり、日本がどれほど、当時の朝鮮を日本と比較できる文化レベルに引き上げようと努力したかについて、数多くの真実が書かれています。

This book, "1907 in Korea with Marquis Ito" written by George Trumbull Ladd provides an excellent description of the landscape and daily lives of people of Seoul and other cities just before the Japanese annexation.

ジョージ・トランブル・ラッド著『1907 IN KOREA WITH MARQUIS ITO（伊藤侯爵と共に朝鮮にて）』は、朝鮮併合前のソウルや他の街の様子、人々の日常生活が紹介された素晴らしい内容です。

Both books are available in Japan in an English-Japanese bilingual edition.

どちらも、日本で日英二ヵ国語版が出版されています。

As for my statements about Korean falsehoods, may I direct you to this newspaper article. "A low-trust society", The Korea Herald English edition. 2011.8.02. The article states frankly that one of the biggest social problems in Korea is lying.

韓国人の嘘の問題については、次の新聞記事を読んでください。"A low-trust society（低信頼社会）" The Korea Herald 英語版（2011 年 8 月 2 日）。この記事は、現在の韓国社会の一番の問題は、嘘をつくこと、絶えず嘘をつき続けていることだ、と率直に書いています。

Concerning the slave salt farms that exist in South Korea today, please read The Independent, "The islands of abuse: Inside South Korea's slave farms for the disabled" January 3, 2015.

現代韓国の塩田での奴隷労働については、英国の新聞インデペンデントの、2015 年 1 月 3 日の記事 "The islands of abuse: Inside South Korea' s slave farms for the disabled（虐待の島：障害者を奴隷のように酷使する韓国の塩田の内実）" を読んでください。

I had my own problems with that aspect of Korea when I lived there. I worked in 3 different Hagwon, or English language school in Korea. They all refused to pay me at the end of the month. The only school that paid me was an American-run school. It was this constant problem that caused me to leave Korea and return to Japan.

私が韓国に住んでいたとき、同様の問題を実際に体験しました。私が働いた 3 ヵ所のハグァン（英会話学校）で働きましたが、月末に給与を支払ってくれませんでした。ちゃんと給与を支払ったのは、アメリカ人が経営する学校だけでした。こういうことがよくあったので、私は韓国を去り、日本に戻りました。

I have seen U.S. Department of State's travel advisory that one should not believe any Korean person about working conditions in a Korean English school. Only believe another American who has worked there.

アメリカ外務省の渡航者勧告で、韓国の英会話学校で仕事をする場合、仕事の条件について韓国人の話を信じてはいけないというのを見たことがあります。信用できるのは、その学校で働いたことがあるアメリカ人だけだという訳です。

But I sincerely hope that Koreans can outgrow these wild fantasies about the war, and find a way to cooperate with Japanese people for the future.

私が切に願うのは、韓国人が大東亜戦争の被害妄想から脱却し、将来のために日本人と互いに協力する道を模索してほしい、ということです。

But I will wait and see.

なり行きを見守ろうと思います。

I sincerely hope that Americans can stop complaining about Japan then and the Pacific War. But since Americans are still arguing about their own Civil War of 150 years ago, I am not optimistic about this.

また私は、アメリカ人が当時の日本や大東亜戦争を批判するのをやめてほしい、と思っています。しかし、アメリカ人は今も150年前の南北戦争について論争しているくらいですから、これに関しては悲観的です。

We are heading for a dark future with limited resources. Now it is time for Japan to recreate the society Japan had in the Edo era, where people had confidence in their own country and culture, and everybody had a place and function within society. Things were used and reused, and the Japanese concept "Mottainai" was thought highly of. We must stop being attracted by foreign philosophies, such as the American idea that a huge wealth gap is a good idea, a matter of course.

世界は資源が乏しくなる暗い将来に向かっています。日本は江戸時代のような社会を取り戻すべきです。江戸時代、人々は自分たちの文化に自信を持ち、社会の中でそれぞれの立場で機能していました。物が再利用され、「もったいない」という哲学が大切にされていました。外国の哲学、たとえば、大きな資産格差があるのは当たり前で良いことだ、というアメリカ人みたいな考えはやめるべきです。

America is tipping into a Civil War. Instead, Japan should lead the world by example, and show other countries how to prosper in these difficult times ahead.

アメリカは現在内乱へと向かっています。これから迎える前途多難の時代をどう乗り越えるか、日本は他国の手本となって世界を導かなければなりません。

And my thanks to many more people I have no space to mention here, who helped make this book possible.

　この本は、ここに書き切れないほどたくさんの方々の協力があり、出版することができました。心から感謝しています。

マックス・フォン・シュラー

Afterward to the second edition
普及版刊行に寄せて

Since I first wrote this book seven years ago, the world has changed greatly. It has become obvious that America and the West in general are in steep decline. In the Meiji era, Japan took an independent road, to protect itself from encroachment from Western powers. These countries are now failing. Basically, they became too arrogant, too lazy, felt too entitled.

この本を最初に書いた７年前以来、世界は大きく変わりました。アメリカや欧米諸国全般が急速に衰退していることは明らかです。明治時代、日本は欧米列強の侵略から自国を守るため、独立の道を歩みました。これらの国々は今、失敗しています。基本的に、彼らはあまりにも傲慢になり、あまりにも怠惰になり、あまりにも権利を感じすぎるようになりました。

Being born in America, I can comment on that country. For the 49 years I lived in Japan, Japanese people would tell me I come from a free country. Well, America has never been free. Politically yes, but not socially.

アメリカで生まれた私は、アメリカについてコメント出来ます。日本に住んでいた49年間、日本人は私に自由の国から来たと言いました。しかし、アメリカは決して自由ではなかったです。政治的にはそうだが、社会的にはそうではありません。

New immigrants would always have to fight for a place in

society. Yet, it was true that if you worked hard, you could achieve economic success in America. And with that, basic social acceptance.

新移民は常に社会での居場所を求めて戦わなければならないです。しかし、懸命に働けば、アメリカで経済的成功を収めることができるのは事実でした。そしてそれとともに、基本的な社会的受容も得られるのです。

Actually, I have found Japanese people to be much more socially accepting than America ever was. In 49 years, I can say I have experienced extremely few instances of actual prejudice in Japan.

実際、私は日本人がアメリカよりもずっと社会的に受け入れられていると感じています。この49年間、日本で実際に偏見を感じたことはほとんどありません。

However, in the last 50 years, many Americans have changed. They feel entitled. They believe they should have success simply by being born. They grew up in a permissive society, and felt they could do what ever they pleased. Schools became weak, taught them they were wonderful just by being born.

しかし、この50年間で多くのアメリカ人は変わりました。彼らは権利を与えられたと感じています。生まれただけで成功するはずだと信じています。彼らは寛容な社会で育ち、何をやっても許されると感じています。学校は弱くなり、生まれただけで素晴らしいと教えるようになりました。

Now we have the rise of victim culture. That is why the Transgender movement has exploded so much. Racial and ethnic minorities experienced harsh prejudice in the past. Yet slavery for Black people ended 158 years ago. Yes, prejudice still lingered. But the America of today is very different from that older America.

今は被害者文化が台頭しています。だからこそ、トランスジェンダー運動がこれほどまでに爆発しました。人種的、民族的マイノリティは過去に厳しい偏見を経験しました。しかし、黒人の奴隷制度は158年前に終わりました。たしかに偏見はまだ残っていました。しかし、今のアメリカはその昔のアメリカとはまったく違います。

The decline of America is not the result of some Russian or Chinese plan. It is completely created by Americans, Made in USA. American Communists and other deep Leftists decided to follow Herbert Marcuse, of the Frankfurt school, and use sexual and racial minorities to create Communist revolution in America. They have had great success.

アメリカの衰退は、ロシアや中国の計画の結果ではありません。完全にアメリカ人が作り出したものであり、メイド・イン・USAなのです。アメリカの共産主義者やその他の深層左翼は、フランクフルト学派のハーバート・マルクーゼに倣い、性的マイノリティや人種的マイノリティを利用してアメリカに共産主義革命を起こそうと決めました。彼らは大成功を収めました。

In 1975, when I was a US Marine, I was an undercover Naval

Intelligence inside an America Communist spy cell in Iwakuni Japan. I remember that they targeted the wives of US Marines, telling them they were sexually exploited.

私が米海兵隊員だった1975年、私は海軍情報部の潜入捜査官として、岩国にあるアメリカ共産主義者のスパイ組織に潜入していました。彼らは米海兵隊員の妻をターゲットにし、性的搾取を受けていると言っていたことを覚えています。

The Communist Left also created the Transgender movement, to create a sexual minority that would be very vocal and violent. They have succeeded in creating a movement with many Black Americans, that they are entitled to compensation because of slavery, and that rioting, looting and other crimes are okay.

共産主義左派はトランスジェンダー運動も起こし、声高で暴力的な性的マイノリティを作り上げました。彼らは多くのアメリカ黒人に、奴隷制度があるから補償を受ける権利があり、暴動や略奪、その他の犯罪は構わないという運動を作り出すことに成功しました。

The traditional conservative Right is finally starting to wake up to what is happening. There is pushback on sexual education in schools that encourages children to become Transgender.

伝統的な保守右派は、ようやく何が起きているかに目覚め始めています。子どもたちにトランスジェンダーになることを奨励するような学校での性教育に反発があります。

But this process will be very violent. Basically, it will be city people against rural people. It will be fought in the suburbs of American big cities. It has already begun. With Left wing governments in all American big cities and left wing policies, crime, homelessness, and drug use has greatly increased.

しかし、このプロセスは非常に暴力的なものになるだろう。基本的には、都会の人々と農村の人々が戦うことになります。アメリカの大都市の郊外で戦われることになります。それはすでに始まっています。アメリカのすべての大都市で左翼政権が誕生し、左翼的な政策によって、犯罪、ホームレス、薬物使用が大幅に増加しています。

Retail outlets are abandoning the big cities, urban gangs are already raiding retail outlets in the suburbs. Police have been greatly weakened by Left wing municipal governments, they cannot control the situation.

商売店は大都市を見捨て、都市部の暴力団はすでに郊外の小売店を襲っています。警察は左翼自治体によって大幅に弱体化し、状況をコントロールできなくなっています。

Yet in the rural areas, and suburbs, Right wing militias do exist. Many of them. The battle of America is now going to be fought.

しかし、地方や郊外には右翼の民兵が存在します。その数は多いです。アメリカの戦いはこれからです。

Sometimes Japanese people ask me what they can do to help America. My answer is nothing. We must save Japan. Americans have a deep desire to force other nations to accept their ideas.

Many Left wing activists, including the present American ambassador, are working hard to promote Leftist sexual customs among Japanese people.

ときどき日本人に、アメリカを助けるために何ができるかと聞かれます。私の答えは「何もない」です。私たちは日本を救わなければならないです。アメリカ人は他国に自分たちの考えを受け入れさせたいという願望が深いです。現在のアメリカ大使を含む多くの左翼活動家が、日本人に左翼的な性風俗を広めようと懸命に働いています。

We must resist this. In fact, without American ideas of sexual politics, Japan is the most sexually free, liberated nation on earth. American policies are designed to create social chaos. We must save Japan from America.

我々はこれに抵抗しなければなりません。実際、アメリカの性政治に関する考え方がなければ、日本は地球上で最も性的に自由で解放された国です。アメリカの政策は、社会の混乱を引き起こすように設計されています。私たちは日本をアメリカから救わねばなりません。

At the time of this writing, the Japanese government is seeking to deepen ties with the West. The government wants to bring many foreigners into Japan. This is a mistake. We should revive the spirit that led Japan to create the East Asia Co-Prosperity sphere. If we do not strongly and decisively split off from the West, Japan will be destroyed. The West has chosen their fate, to fall into ruin. We should not share that fate, but create our own destiny.

この本を書いている時点で、日本政府は欧米との関係を深めようとしています。政府は多くの外国人を日本に呼び込もうとしています。これは間違いです。日本が大東亜共栄圏を作り上げた精神を復活させるべきです。強く、断固として欧米と決別しなければ、日本は滅びてしまいます。欧米は破滅する運命を選びました。我々はその運命を共有するのではなく、自らの運命を切り開くべきです。

Notes

注記

※以下、本文中で使用される用語についての説明です。

◆「李氏朝鮮」は朝鮮併合以前の朝鮮半島を意味します（大韓帝国も含みます）。
◆「朝鮮」、「当時の朝鮮」は朝鮮併合時代の朝鮮半島を意味します。
◆「北朝鮮」、「韓国」は現在の朝鮮半島の二つの国を意味します。
◆「コリア」、「コリアン」は南北両国家国民、あるいは将来統一された後の国家国民を意味します。

List of Reference Literature
参考文献

The New Korea

著者：Alleyne Ireland
出版：E. P. Dutton Japanese translation Sakuranohana
邦題：朝鮮が劇的に豊かになった時代
日英対訳：桜の花出版（2013）

This work is a must for anyone studying the Japanese-Korean relationship. It provides an extremely detailed scholarly account of Japanese development of Korea.

この本は日韓問題の研究のためには絶対必要です。詳細かつ学術的に日本の朝鮮併合時代の朝鮮開発を説明しています。

1907 in Korea with Marquis Ito

著者：George Trumbull Ladd
出版：Longmans, Green & Co.
邦題：1907　伊藤侯爵と共に朝鮮にて
日英対訳：桜の花出版（2015）

Mr. Ladd spent several months in Korea on the eve of annexation, and gives an interesting account of Korean society and life at that time.

ラッド氏は併合直前に数ヵ月朝鮮を旅しました。彼の当時の朝鮮の社会と生活の話はとても面白いです。

Getting Over It!

著者：Sonfa Oh（呉善花）
出版：Tachibana Publishing
邦題：なぜ「反日韓国に未来はない」のか
出版：小学館新書（2013）

A very good description of how anti-Japanese education was promoted in the postwar years, how the anti-Japanese relationship evolved in Korea, and the dangers for Korea in the future of this course.

戦後の韓国における反日教育の推進を説明することで、韓国人の反日思想がどのように進化していったかを解説しています。この状況がなぜ韓国の未来にとって危険であるか、はっきりと警鐘を鳴らしています。

America encounters Japan

著者 :William Louis Neumann
出版 :Torchbooks
邦題：アメリカと日本—ペリーからマッカーサーまで
出版：研究社出版（1986）

A very good account of the prewar years. It details the efforts of American Christian missionaries to aid China and Christianize it, panic about Japan from Californians, and the efforts of the FDR administration to force Japan into starting war.

戦前について書いている良い本です。中国を援助しキリスト教化するアメリカのキリスト教宣教師団のこと、カリフォルニアに由来する日本に関わるパニック、フランクリン・D・ルーズベルト政権が日本を戦争に追い込んだことについて詳しく書かれています。

Soldiers of the Sun: The rise and fall of the Imperial Japanese Army

著者 :Meirion Harries
出版 :Random House

A history of the Japanese Imperial Army. The notation of only 17 military police at Nanking is on page 230.

大日本帝国陸軍の歴史について書かれた本です。特筆すべきポイントとして、南京事件当時、南京には憲兵が17人しかいなかったということが230ページに書かれています。

Day of Deceit The truth about FDR and Pearl Harbor

著者 :Robert Stinnett
出版 :Touchstone
邦題：真珠湾の真実 — ルーズベルト欺瞞の日々
出版：文藝春秋（2001）

The FDR administration's 8 points plan to force Japan into starting war is on page 8. The book details how the FDR administration knew the attack on Pearl Harbor was coming.

フランクリン・D・ルーズベルト政権が日本を戦争に追い込

んだ８つの計画を８ページに書いています。この本は、ルーズベルト政権がどのように事前に真珠湾攻撃を知っていたかについて説明しています。

Embracing Defeat: Japan in the wake of WWII

著者 :John W. Dower
出版 :Norton
邦題：敗北を抱きしめて―第二次大戦後の日本人（上・下）
出版：岩波書店（2004）

Explains how the Tokyo War Crimes trials were extremely unfair, totally unjust.

東京裁判がいかに極端に不公平で完全に不公正なものだったのかを説明している本です。

War without Mercy: Pacific War

著者 :John W. Dower
出版 :PANTEON BOOKS
邦題：容赦なき戦争―太平洋戦争における人種差別
出版：平凡社（2001）

Describes the propaganda efforts of Japan and the US in the war. Also mentions how US troops killed 50% of surrendering Japanese troops.

戦争中の日本とアメリカのプロパガンダについて説明しています。また、米軍が投降しようとする日本兵の半数を如何に殺害したかが書かれています。

What Soldiers Do: Sex and the American GI in France

著者 :Mary Louise Roberts
出版 :Chicago
邦題：兵士とセックス―第二次世界大戦下のフランスで米兵は何をしたのか？
出版：明石書店（2015）

Describes how American troops raped, pillaged and forcefully bought women for sex across France in WWII. Also mentions the American Comfort Women system in Hawaii in WWII.

第二次世界大戦でアメリカ兵が如何に女性をレイプし、略奪し、売春をさせるためにフランス中を強制的に連れ回したかを説明しています。そして、アメリカのハワイの慰安婦システムについても書かれています。

This Kind of War

著者 :T. R. Fehrenbach
出版 :Macmillian

Describes the lack of morale and fighting ability of the US 2nd infantry division in the Korean war, when faced with difficulty. Also describes the collapse of American society among US POWs in Korea.

困難に直面した時の朝鮮戦争での米第２歩兵師団の士気と戦

闘能力の欠如について分析しています。実に、朝鮮における米兵捕虜社会の崩壊について説明しています。

A Republic, Not an Empire: Reclaiming America's Destiny

著者 :Patrick J. Buchanan
出版 :Regnery Publishing, Inc.

He well describes the extensive compromises offered by Prime minister Konoye, such as withdrawal from Indo China and the bulk of China. The Japanese wish was that then America would lift the economic embargo. Yet Secretary of State Cordell Hull refused this, because he felt that it was not enough. Truly, the Roosevelt administration wanted war.

近衛文麿総理大臣が申し出た対米戦争回避のための広範な妥協案について説明しています。インドシナと大部分の中国からの撤退などです。日本が求めていたのはアメリカの経済制裁解除でした。しかし米国務長官のコーデル・ハルがこの妥協案は十分ではないと拒否しました。やはりルーズベルト政権は開戦を望んでいたということがわかります。

John Toland' books

All of his works on WWII are illuminating. They provide a sympathetic view of Japan's war effort.

彼の第二次世界大戦に関する作品は全て啓発的です。著作は日本の戦争努力に同情的な見方をしています。

◆著者◆

マックス・フォン・シュラー（Max von Schuler）

本名、マックス・フォン・シュラー小林。
元海兵隊・歴史研究家。ドイツ系アメリカ人。
1974年岩国基地に米軍海兵隊として来日、その後日本、韓国で活動。
退役後、国際基督教大学、警備会社を経て、役者として「釣りバカ日誌８」等、ナレーターとして「足立美術館音声ガイド」等、日本で活動。
YouTube公式チャンネル「軍事歴史がMAXわかる！」でも情報発信中。
著書に『アメリカ人が語る 内戦で崩壊するアメリカ』『アメリカ人が語る日本の歴史　日本に迫る統一朝鮮(コリア)の悪夢』（ともにハート出版）、『太平洋戦争 アメリカに嵌められた日本』（ワック）、『アメリカ白人の闇』（桜の花出版）、『アメリカはクーデターによって、社会主義国家になってしまった』（青林堂）などがある。

編集協力：石井　修

[普及版] アメリカ人が語るアメリカが隠しておきたい日本の歴史

令和５年10月29日　第１刷発行
令和６年２月14日　第４刷発行

著　者　マックス・フォン・シュラー
発行者　日高裕明
発　行　株式会社ハート出版
〒171-0014 東京都豊島区池袋 3-9-23
TEL.03(3590)6077　FAX.03(3590)6078
ハート出版ホームページ　https://www.810.co.jp

定価はカバーに表示してあります。

ISBN978-4-8024-0162-3　C0021

印刷･サンケイ総合印刷株式会社